OLYMPIC TALES

A JOURNEY THROUGH TIME, TRIUMPH AND TEARS

Copyright © 2024 by Ezra Flint

All rights reserved. No part of this publication may be reproduced, distributed, or transmitted in any form or by any means, including photocopying, recording, or other electronic or mechanical methods, without the prior written permission of the publisher except as permitted by U.S. copyright law.

CONTENTS

Introduction 5

Ancient Games 9

    Myths and Legends 11

    Extreme Sports 17

    Super Athletes 25

    Anecdotes and Curiosities 31

Modern games 35

    Introduction to Modern Games 37

    Legends of the Olympic Games 41

    Paralympic Games 67

    Women in the Olympic Games 71

    The First Winter Olympics 79

    Symbolism of Medals 83

    Opening Ceremonies 87

    Olympic Mascots and Their Significance 91

    Controversy and Scandals 95

    Anecdotes in the Games 101

    Olympic Athletes Who Became Movie Stars 109

INTRODUCTION

The Olympic Games are more than just a sporting competition; they are a voyage through time, culture, and the history of humanity. From their origins in ancient Greece to their modern-day global spectacle, the Games have been a symbol of unity, effort, and personal achievement.

In ancient Greece around 776 BC, the Olympic Games were born. Held in the city of Olympia every four years, these religious and sporting events brought together athletes from different Greek city-states to compete in honor of Zeus, the king of the gods. More than just a competition, the Olympic Games represented a temporary truce in hostilities between the city-states, fostering unity and cultural exchange.

After centuries of splendor, the Olympic Games were interrupted in the 4th century AD by the Roman emperor Theodosius I, who considered them a pagan practice. It was not until the late 19th century, thanks to the efforts of French baron Pierre de Coubertin, that the Olympic Games were revived in Athens in 1896.

Inspired by the ideals of ancient Greece, Coubertin sought to create a sporting event that would promote peace, understanding, and the physical and moral development of young people. With the motto "Citius, altius, fortius" (Faster, higher, stronger), the modern Olympic Games became an international benchmark for sporting excellence.

In an increasingly globalized and diverse world, the Olympic Games take on even greater significance. Beyond the sporting competition, the Games represent an opportunity to:

- Foster peace and understanding between nations: Bringing together athletes from all over the world under one flag, the Olympic Games promote dialogue, respect, and tolerance between different cultures.

- Celebrate human excellence: The Olympic Games are a showcase for the talent and dedication of athletes who strive to reach the pinnacle of sporting performance.

- Inspire new generations: The Olympic values of effort, discipline, and personal improvement serve as a role model for children and young people around the world.

- Promote sustainable development: Host cities of the Olympic Games have the opportunity to implement sustainable practices and leave a positive legacy for future generations.

In short, the Olympic Games are much more than just a sporting competition. They are a symbol of hope, unity, and progress that reminds us of the potential we have as human beings to achieve great things and build a better world.

ANCIENT GAMES

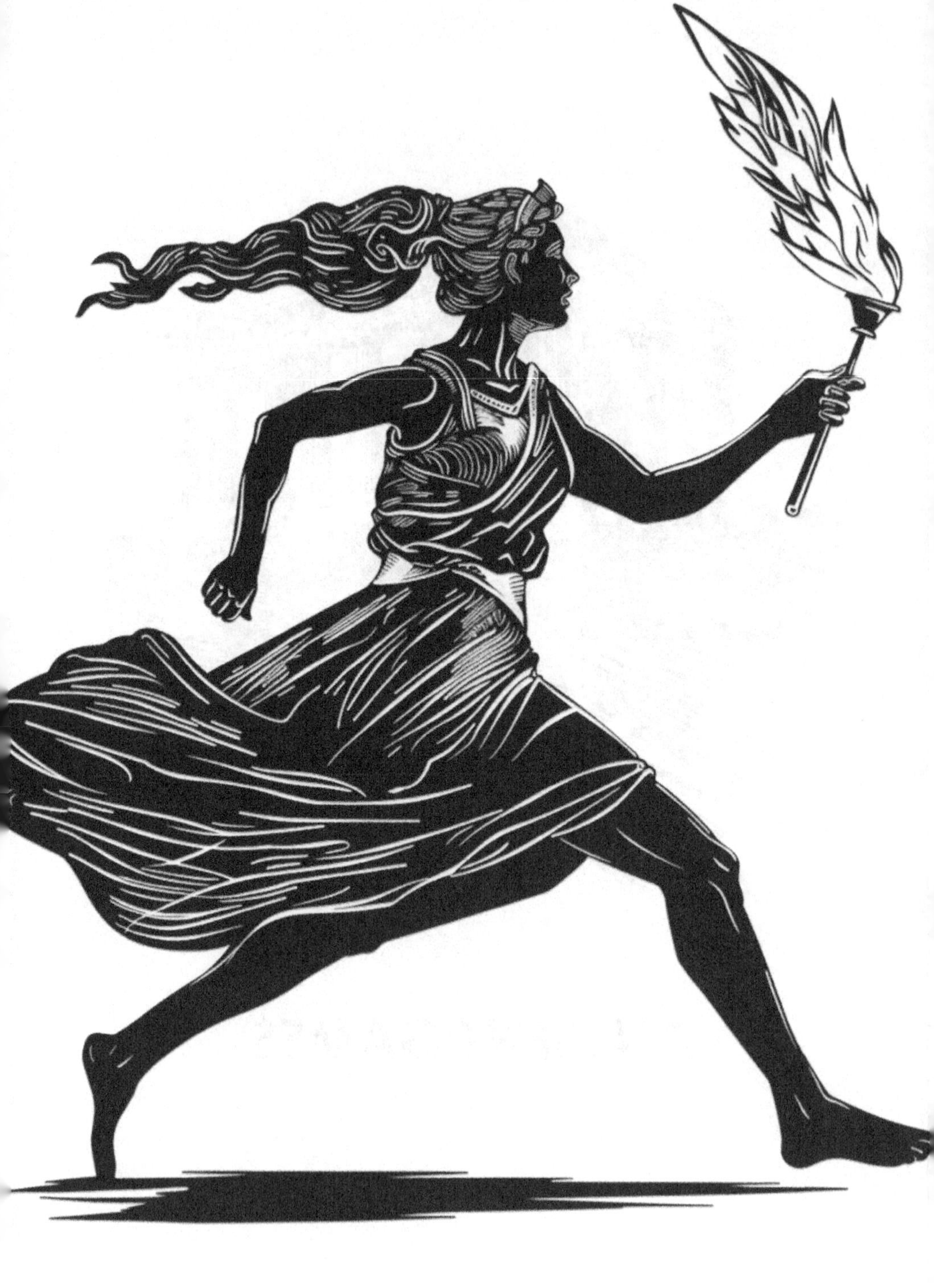

Myths and Legends

Origin of the Games

According to legend, it was Hercules himself, the strongest hero in Greek mythology, who founded the Olympic Games. After completing his Twelve Labors, Hercules organized a competition among his brothers to celebrate his victory over the fearsome Nemean lion. The games were held in Olympia at the foot of Mount Olympus, home of the gods.

Atalanta: The Invincible Runner

Atalanta, a young huntress of extraordinary speed, was known for her cunning and her refusal to marry. Suitors who challenged her to a race risked their lives if they did not defeat her. However, Hippomenes, a young man in love, devised a plan: during the race, he threw three golden apples that Atalanta stopped to pick up, distracting her long enough for him to catch up and beat her.

Cleo and the Olympic Torch

The Olympic torch, a symbol of unity and peace during the Games, also has its own legend. Cleo, a priestess of Artemis, was responsible for lighting the first torch with the sun's rays at the top of Mount Olympus. It is said that she ran to Olympia without rest, carrying the sacred flame that would illuminate the games.

Theseus: An Olympic Hero

In ancient Greece, the Athenian hero Theseus, after defeating the Minotaur, went to Olympia to compete in the Olympic Games. The competition was fierce, but Theseus, confident in his strength and cunning, faced the best wrestlers in Greece. Fight after fight, Theseus advanced, leaving his rivals behind. The crowd cheered him on, admiring his skill and courage. Finally, in the final after a tough battle, Theseus was proclaimed the winner of the pankration, consecrating his victory as a symbol of strength, bravery, and determination for Athens.

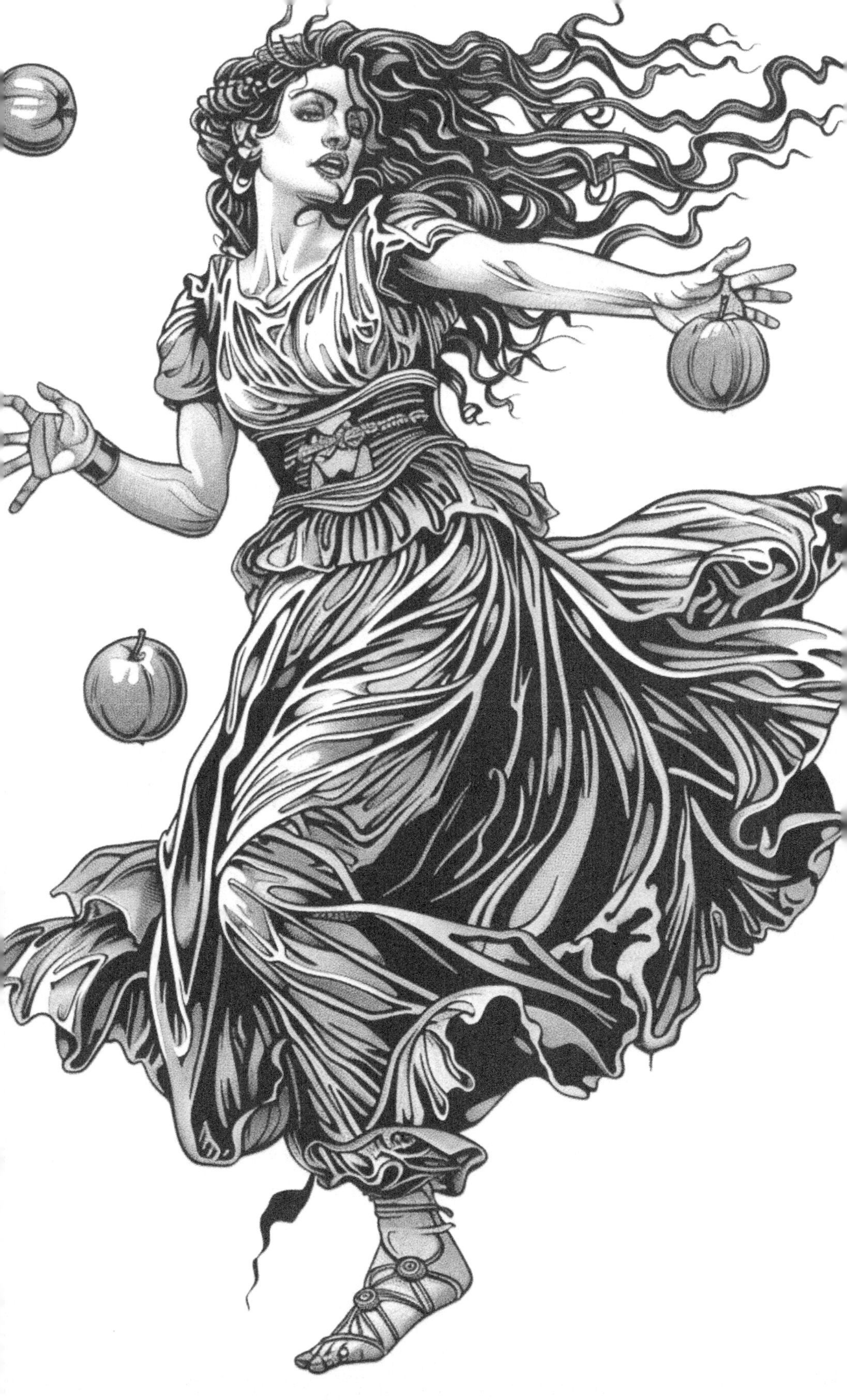

Pelops and Hippodamia: A Race with a Cheat

Pelops, a young suitor of Princess Hippodamia, was not the strongest, but he was the most cunning. To win the princess's hand in a chariot race, he bribed his rival's charioteer, Oenomaus, to sabotage his chariot. With this trick, Pelops claimed victory and married Hippodamia, but the curse of Oenomaus would haunt them forever.

The Gods at the Games

The Greek gods also participated in the Olympic Games, although they did not do so openly. They often disguised themselves as mortals to compete with each other and demonstrate their skills. Zeus, the king of the gods, was a great fan of wrestling, while Apollo, the god of the sun and music, was known for his archery skills.

Coroebus the First Olympic Champion

According to legend, Coroebus, a cook from Elis, was the first athlete to win a race at the Olympic Games. It is said that while preparing a meal for the athletes, he saw that the competition was about to begin, and without a second thought, took off his clothes and ran onto the track. Thanks to his physical condition and his cunning, Coroebus won the victory, becoming a legend and starting the long tradition of Olympic champions.

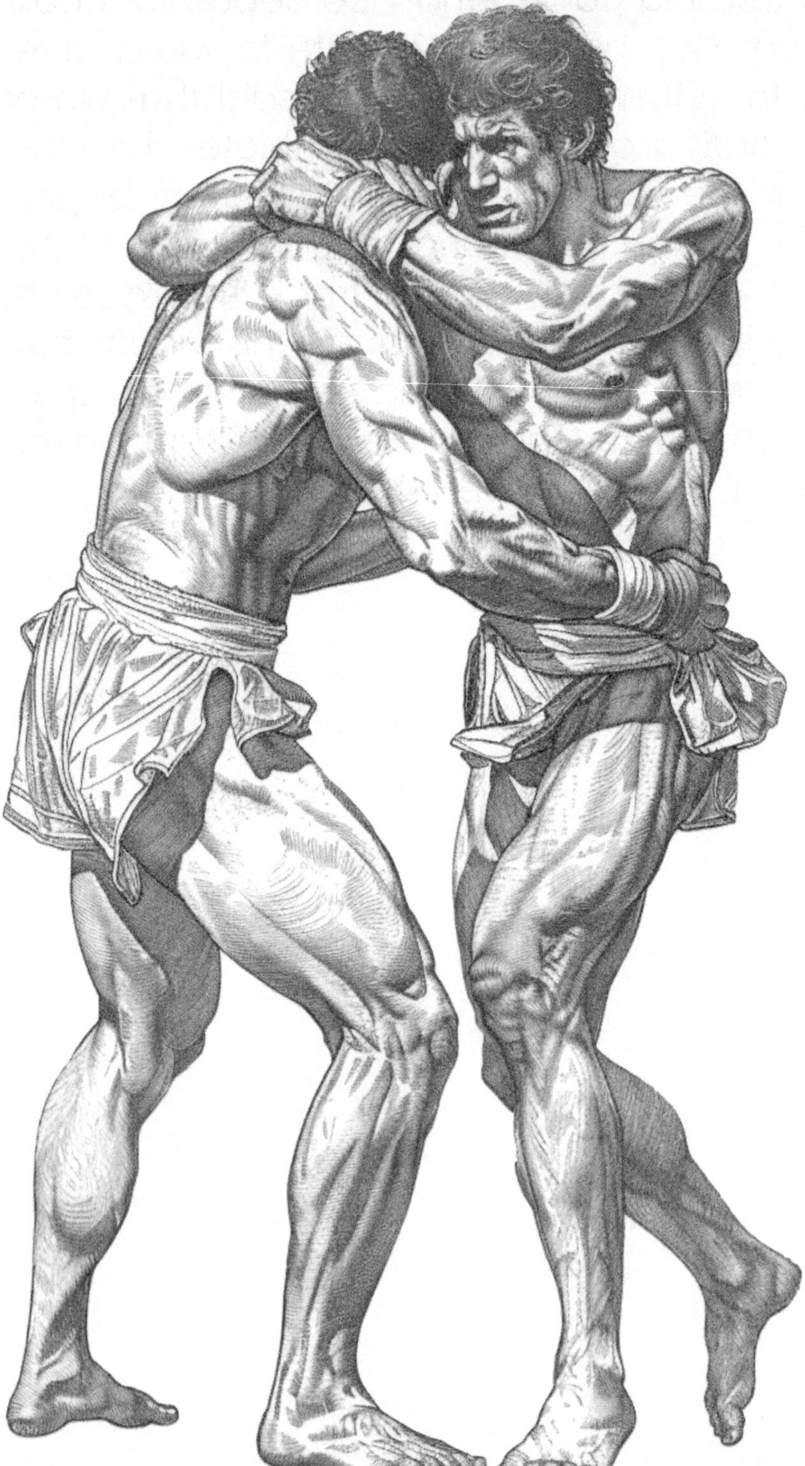

Extreme Sports

Imagine a time when athletes didn't just compete for glory but also faced wild bulls, ran barefoot on uneven terrain, and threw discuses the size of a plate. Yes, you read that right! The Olympic Games in ancient Greece were an epic spectacle full of disciplines that today would seem crazy to us, but that at that time were the ultimate challenge for the bravest athletes.

The King of Speed: The Foot Race (Stadion)

Forget about tartan tracks and sneakers. In ancient Greece, runners competed barefoot on a 192-meter dirt track called the "stadion". The distance was short, but the intensity was brutal. The athletes started at the same time, and the first to cross the finish line was the winner. An explosive race where brute strength and technique were key to achieving glory!

The Pentathlon: A Challenge for the Most Complete

Do you think you are a complete athlete? In ancient Greece, the pentathlon was the ultimate test to prove your worth. This discipline combined five events: the foot race (stadion), the long jump, the javelin throw, the discus throw, and wrestling. A challenge that demanded endurance, strength, speed, precision, and, of course, a lot of guts!

Wrestling: A No-Rules Fight

If you like MMA fights, ancient Greek wrestling would leave you breathless. In this discipline, there were no rules or weight limits. Athletes could only use their hands and arms to knock their opponent to the ground three times. A brutal fight where strength, technique, and cunning were the only weapons for victory!

Boxing: One Punch Can Change Everything

In Greek boxing, boxers fought with their fists wrapped in rawhide, making each punch an experience... let's say memorable! There were no rounds or breaks, just two men in the ring until one of them fell or gave up. A high-contact sport where endurance, power, and strategy were essential for survival!

Pankration: The Ultimate Battle

If you thought wrestling and boxing were extreme, wait until you meet pankration! This discipline was a mix of both, where anything was allowed: punches, kicks, strangles... even pulling your beard! There were only two rules: you couldn't bite or gouge your eyes out. A wild and ruthless sport where only the strongest and bravest could emerge victorious!

Chariot Racing: A Crazy Race

Imagine two chariots pulled by four horses at full speed going around an oval track. That's what chariot racing was like in ancient Greece! The drivers, standing on the chariots, had to control the horses, dodge their opponents, and avoid falling from their vehicles. An exciting and dangerous sport where skill, strategy, and a little bit of luck were the keys to winning!

Women's Sports: A Space for Women

Although women could not participate in the original Olympic Games, there were women's sports competitions in ancient Greece. Women practiced running, wrestling, and discus throwing, demonstrating their strength, agility, and skill.

Equestrianism: Mastering a Wild Horse

In ancient Greece, it wasn't just chariot racing. Riders also demonstrated their skills in dressage and jumping competitions. Riding bareback, without a saddle or stirrups, they had to control a wild horse and perform impressive stunts. A sport that required a special connection between the rider and their horse, as well as a lot of courage and control!

Discus and Javelin Throw: Fly High and Far

In ancient Greece, athletes didn't just throw discuses and javelins like they do today. Back then, these objects were much heavier and were thrown using a different technique. The goal was to throw them as far as possible, using strength, technique, and coordination to achieve the greatest distance. A test of power and precision that challenged the limits of the human body!

Pugilato: The Art of Self-Defense

Unlike boxing, pugilato was a discipline more focused on self-defense. Athletes fought with their fists protected by leather gloves filled with hair or horsehair, and the goal was to dodge their opponent's punches and hit them only on the head or torso. A sport that combined strategy, reflexes, and control to emerge victorious without losing composure!

Wrestling: A Hand-to-Hand Combat

In ancient Greece, wrestling was a fundamental discipline for the development of young people. It was practiced in gyms and wrestling schools and was considered a form of training for war. Athletes wrestled hand-to-hand, using holds, throws, and takedowns to defeat their opponent. A sport that demanded strength, technique, and a lot of discipline!

The Modern Pentathlon: A More Modern Version

In modern times, the Olympic pentathlon has been modified to include safer and more accessible disciplines. Instead of wrestling, there is now fencing, swimming, equestrianism, and shooting. However, the essence of the pentathlon remains the same: to test the athletes' strength, endurance, speed, precision, and versatility.

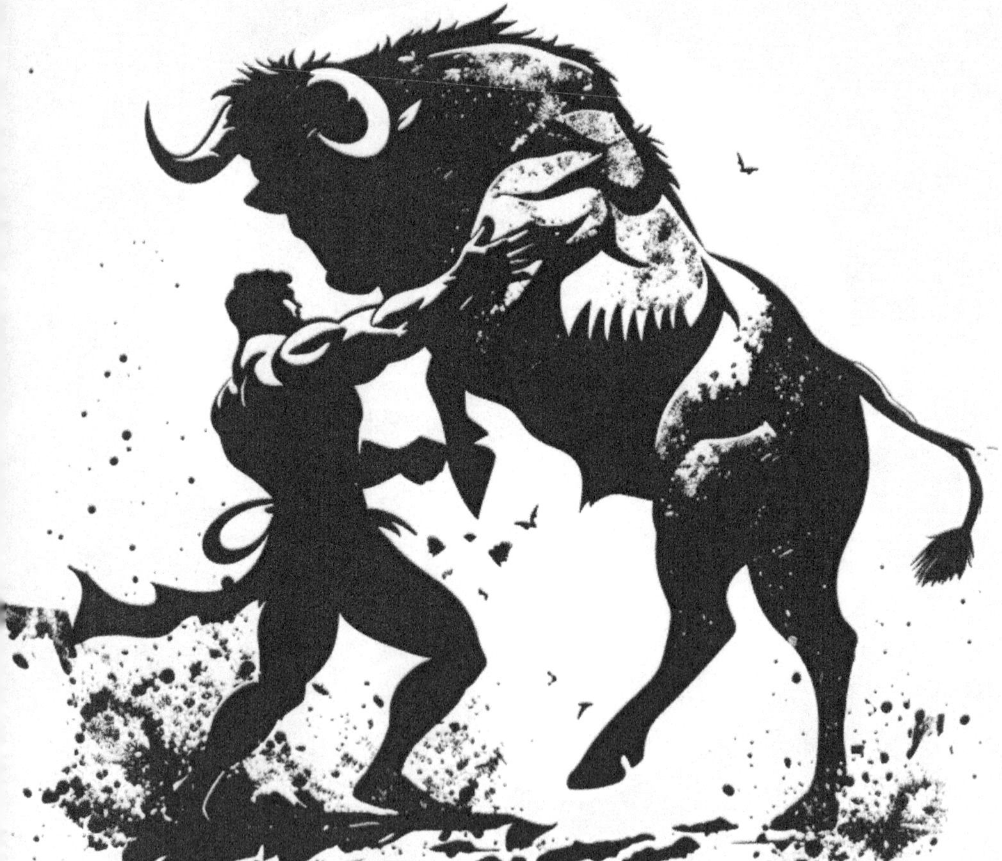

Super Athletes

In ancient Greece, there were not only gods with incredible powers but also athletes who challenged the limits of the human body. Some of them became legends for their sporting feats and their competitive spirit.

Milo of Croton: The Man Who Lifted an Ox

This Greek wrestler was famous for his immense strength. It is said that he trained by carrying a calf on his shoulders until it became an adult ox. A true titan of strength!

Pheidippides: The First Marathoner

In 490 BC, after the Battle of Marathon, a messenger named Pheidippides ran 42 kilometers nonstop from the battlefield to Athens to announce the Greek victory. It is said that upon reaching the city, he only managed to say "Nike!" (Victory!) before collapsing exhausted. A true hero who ran to the limit!

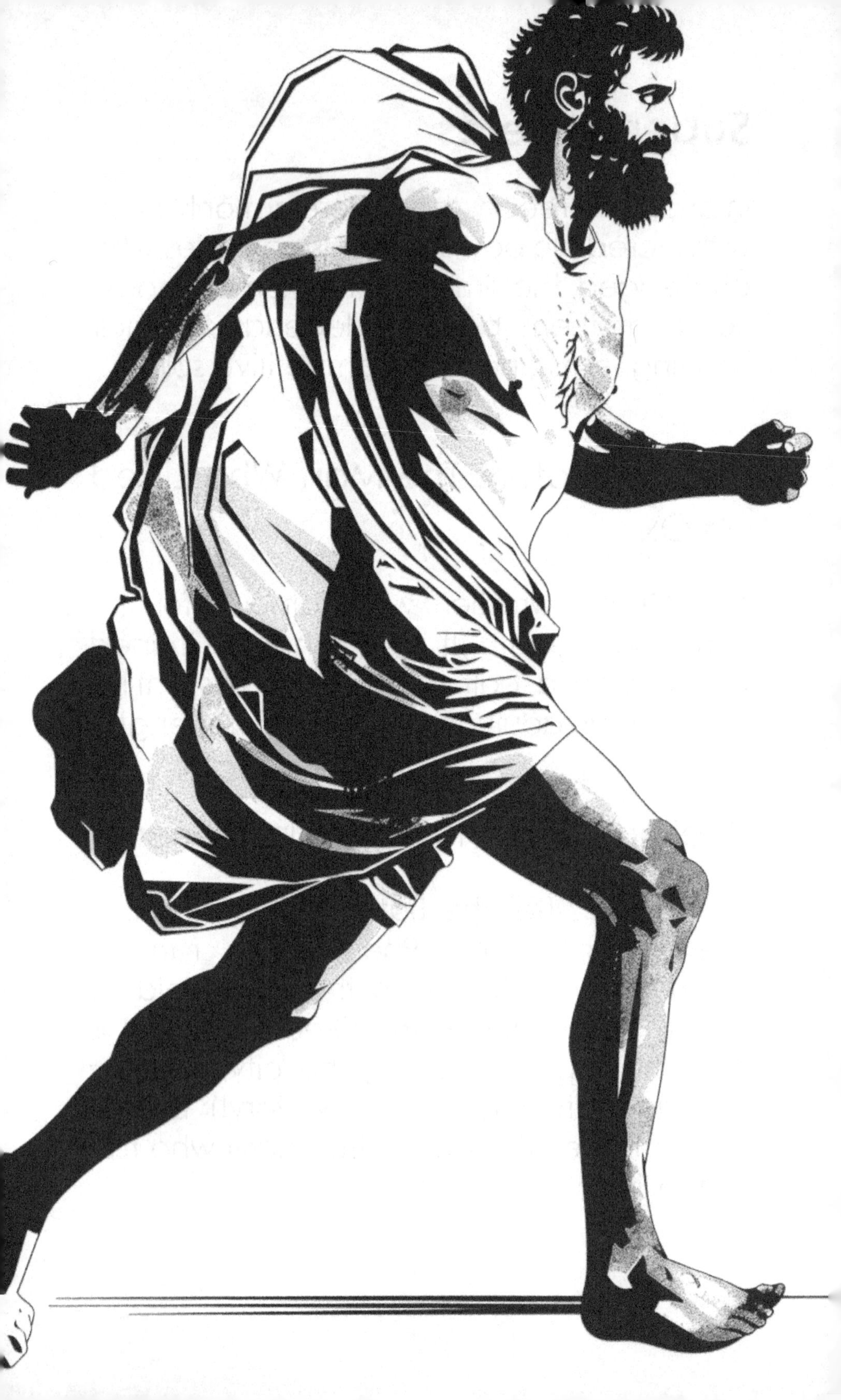

Hippomenes: The Runner Faster Than the Wind

Hippomenes was a young man so fast that he could run faster than the wind. One day, he fell in love with Atalanta, a huntress who would only marry the man who beat her in a race. Hippomenes, desperate to win, resorted to the cunning of the goddess Aphrodite. She gave him three golden apples to throw during the race. Atalanta, distracted by the apples, stopped to pick them up, allowing Hippomenes to win the race. A swift and cunning runner who won the heart of his beloved!

Praxiteles: The Discus Thrower Who Threw the Discus into the Sky

Praxiteles was such a skilled discus thrower that it is said that he once threw the discus so high that it disappeared into the clouds. Spectators were stunned by such a feat, and Praxiteles became an instant legend. A thrower with incredible strength and precision!

Cynisca: The Woman Who Defied the Rules

In ancient Greece, women were not allowed to participate in the Olympics. However, Cynisca was not willing to accept the rules. She secretly trained her horses and entered them in the chariot race under her brother's name. And she won! Cynisca showed that women could compete at the same level as men and became a symbol of the fight for equality.

Diagoras of Rhodes: A Family of Champions

Diagoras of Rhodes was an Olympic boxing champion, but his family legacy is even more impressive. His two sons, Dorieus and Damares, also won gold medals in boxing, and his grandson, Eucles, was a pancration champion. A whole family of champions who showed that athletic talent can be inherited!

Aristocles of Cleonae: The Long-Distance Runner

Aristocles of Cleonae was a long-distance runner specializing in endurance races. It is said that he once ran from Olympia to Sparta, a distance of over 200 kilometers, in a single day! An athlete with exceptional endurance and determination!

Antiochus Epiphanes: The King Who Competed in the Olympics

Antiochus Epiphanes, king of the Seleucid Empire, was a great sports fan. So passionate was he that he decided to compete in the Olympics despite being king. Although he did not win any medals, his participation showed that sport could unite people from different social classes and statuses.

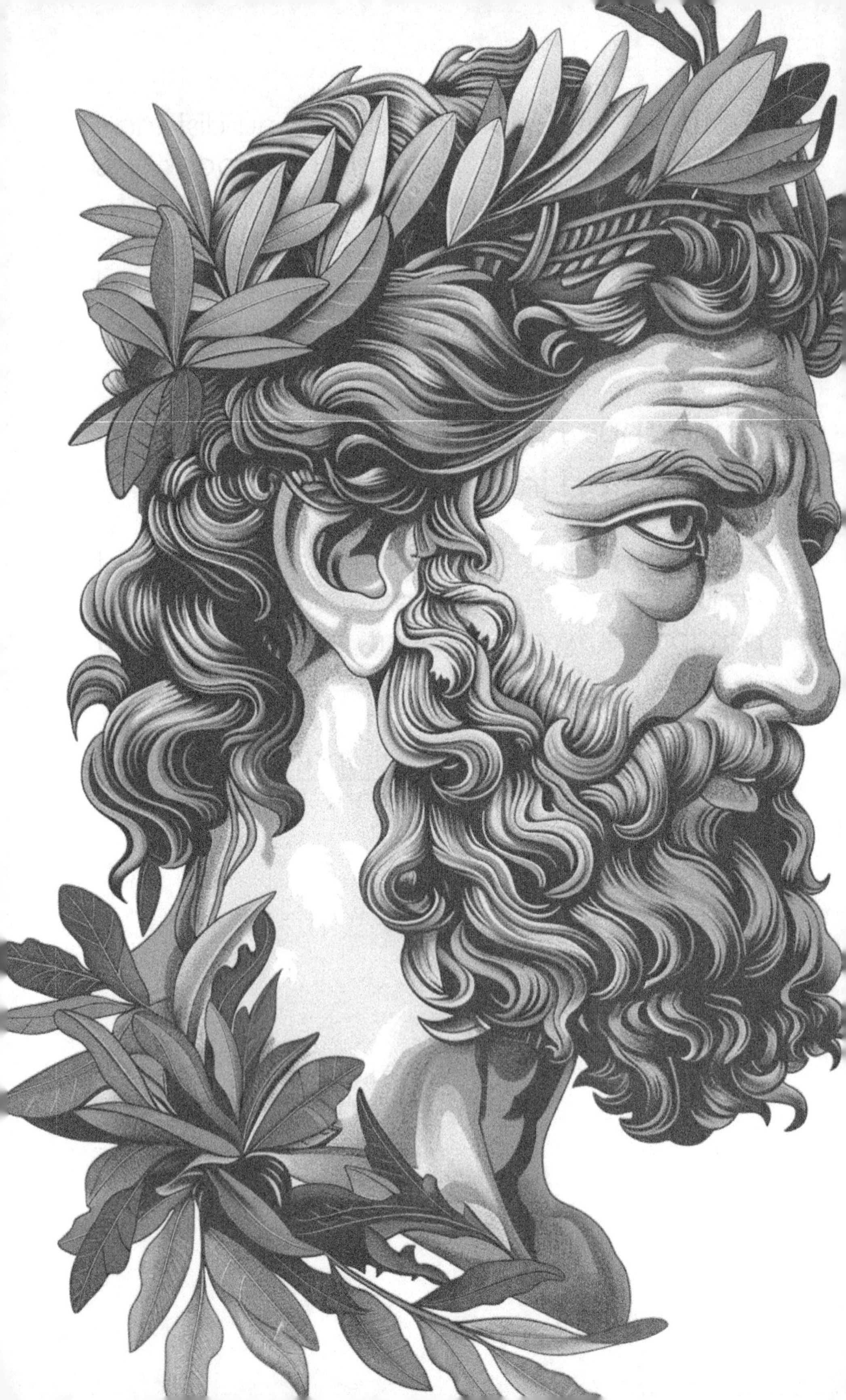

Anecdotes and Curiosities

The Olympic Truce: A Ceasefire for Sport to Flow

Imagine you're in the middle of a war, and suddenly everything stops! Battles were paused during the Olympics so that athletes from conflicting city-states could compete in peace. This sacred truce, known as the "ekecheiria," lasted a month and was an opportunity to unite the Greeks under one symbol: sport. A ceasefire that showed the power of sport to unite even in the most difficult times!

Women Also Competed... But in Disguise!

Although officially women could not participate in the Olympics, some brave athletes defied the rules and competed disguised as men. One of the most famous was Kyniska, who entered her horses in the chariot race under her brother's name and won! Her victory showed that women were capable of competing at the same level as men, even in the face of discriminatory rules.

An Athlete with a Prosthesis: The Champion Who Defied Disability

In ancient Greece, an athlete named Eutimo of Locris competed in the foot race despite having a prosthetic leg. It is said that he was so fast that his rivals did not even realize his disability until the race was over and he took off his prosthesis to celebrate. An example of overcoming adversity that showed that limits are only in the mind!

A Prize... Of Olive Trees

Winners of the Olympic Games did not receive gold, silver, or bronze medals as they do today. Instead, they were awarded a wild olive wreath cut from a sacred tree in the sanctuary of Olympia. This crown was a symbol of honor and prestige and was more precious than any precious metal.

The Athletes Swore by Zeus

Before starting the competitions, all athletes

had to take a solemn oath by Zeus, the king of the gods. In this oath, they promised to compete fairly and honestly, respecting the rules and their opponents. An oath that reflected the values of sportsmanship and fair play that already existed in ancient Greece!

The Athletes Competed Naked

Yes, you read that right. Greek athletes competed completely naked in most of the disciplines. This was considered a way to show respect to the gods and to promote equality among competitors, as wealth or social status did not matter on the field. A custom that today might seem strange to us, but at that time was completely normal!

The Games Lasted Five Days

The ancient Olympic Games were not a one-day event. They lasted for five complete days, during which different sports competitions were held along with religious ceremonies and cultural festivals. A true sporting and cultural marathon!

The Olympic Flame: A Fire That Ignited Passion

In ancient Greece, there was no Olympic torch as we know it today. However, a sacred flame was lit at the sanctuary of Olympia, and this flame symbolized the spirit of the games. The fire was kept burning throughout the event and was extinguished at the end of the competitions.

MODERN GAMES

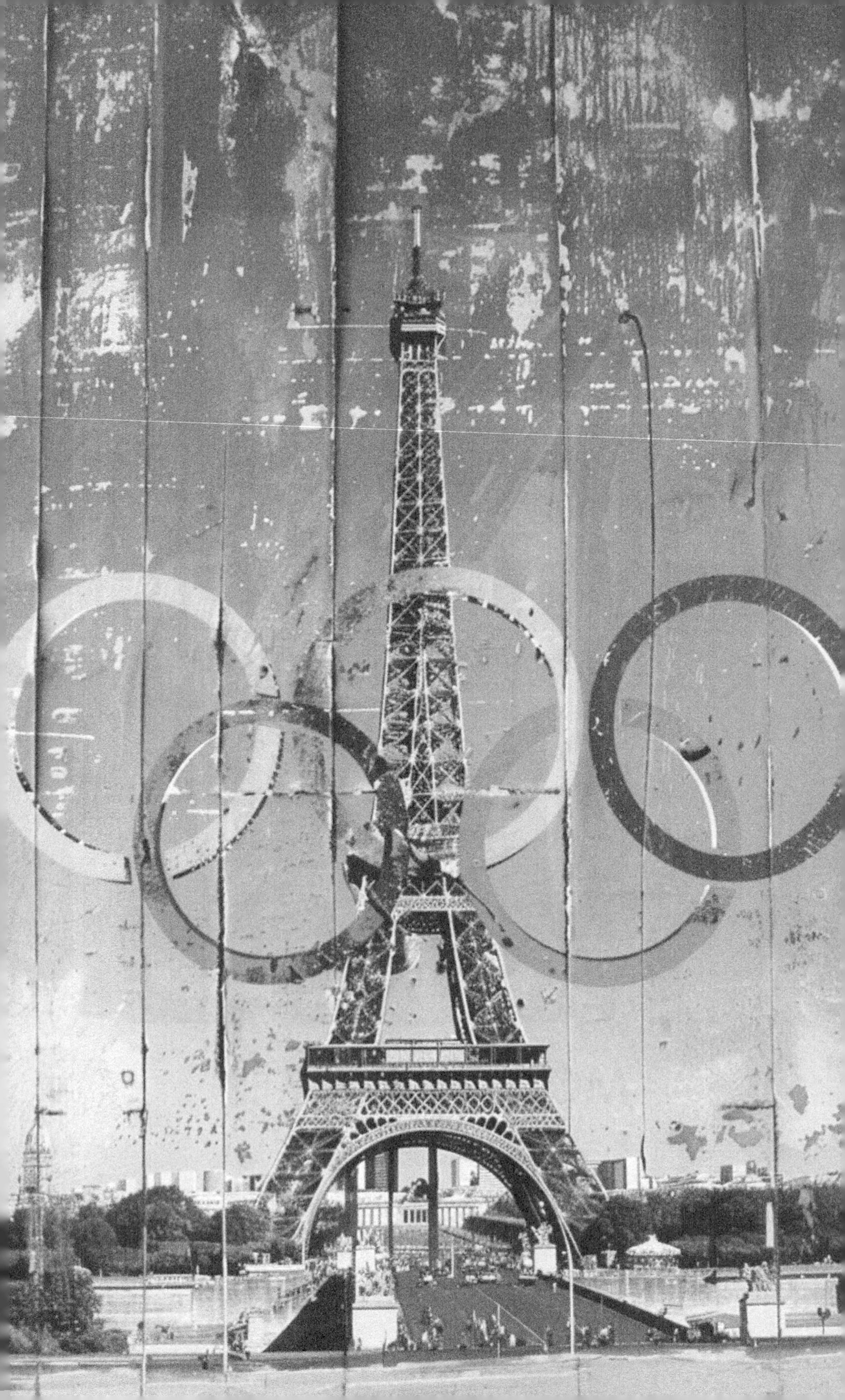

Introduction to Modern Games

The Olympics! A Journey to the Action-Packed Past with Cool Facts for Young Thrill-Seekers Imagine a time warp to Greece in 1896! The world is about to witness something epic: the return of the Olympic Games! After more than 1500 years of absence, the Olympic flame is ignited once again, ready to illuminate the path for athletes from all corners of the globe.

A Cinematic Setting: The Panathinaiko Stadium, constructed in white marble, is the perfect backdrop for this sporting resurrection. Thousands of spectators, filled with anticipation and hearts pounding, fill the stands. Among them, kings, queens, diplomats, and people from all walks of life. The atmosphere is electric!

Athletes from All Over the World: On the track, 241 athletic warriors from 14 countries prepare to compete in 9 different disciplines. Some are Greeks, proud to be the hosts of this historic event. Others hail from places as far-flung as the United States, Australia, or India. It's a true festival of diversity and talent!

A Legendary Marathon: The most important event of the games is the marathon, a 42-kilometer race that tests the endurance and superhuman strength of the athletes. Among them stands out a young Greek postman named Spyros Louis. Barefoot, with his white cap and blue shirt, Louis runs with determination, defying the heat and fatigue.

As he crosses the finish line, Spyros Louis is greeted as a hero. The crowd erupts in cheers and applause. A Greek has won the marathon at the Olympic Games! His victory is a symbol of national pride and the ability to overcome any limit.

A Century of Transformation: The Games of the 20th century were born marked by Pierre de Coubertin's vision: to unite the world through sport. In Athens 1896, only 14 nations and 241 athletes gathered. A century later in Sydney 2000, 201 countries and over 10,000 athletes competed in a globalized event. A giant growth!

Wars and Resurrections: The World Wars forced a hiatus on the Games in 1916, 1940, and 1944. But they were reborn stronger than ever, becoming a symbol of peace and hope. However, politics interfered in 1980 and 1984 with boycotts by Eastern and Western countries.

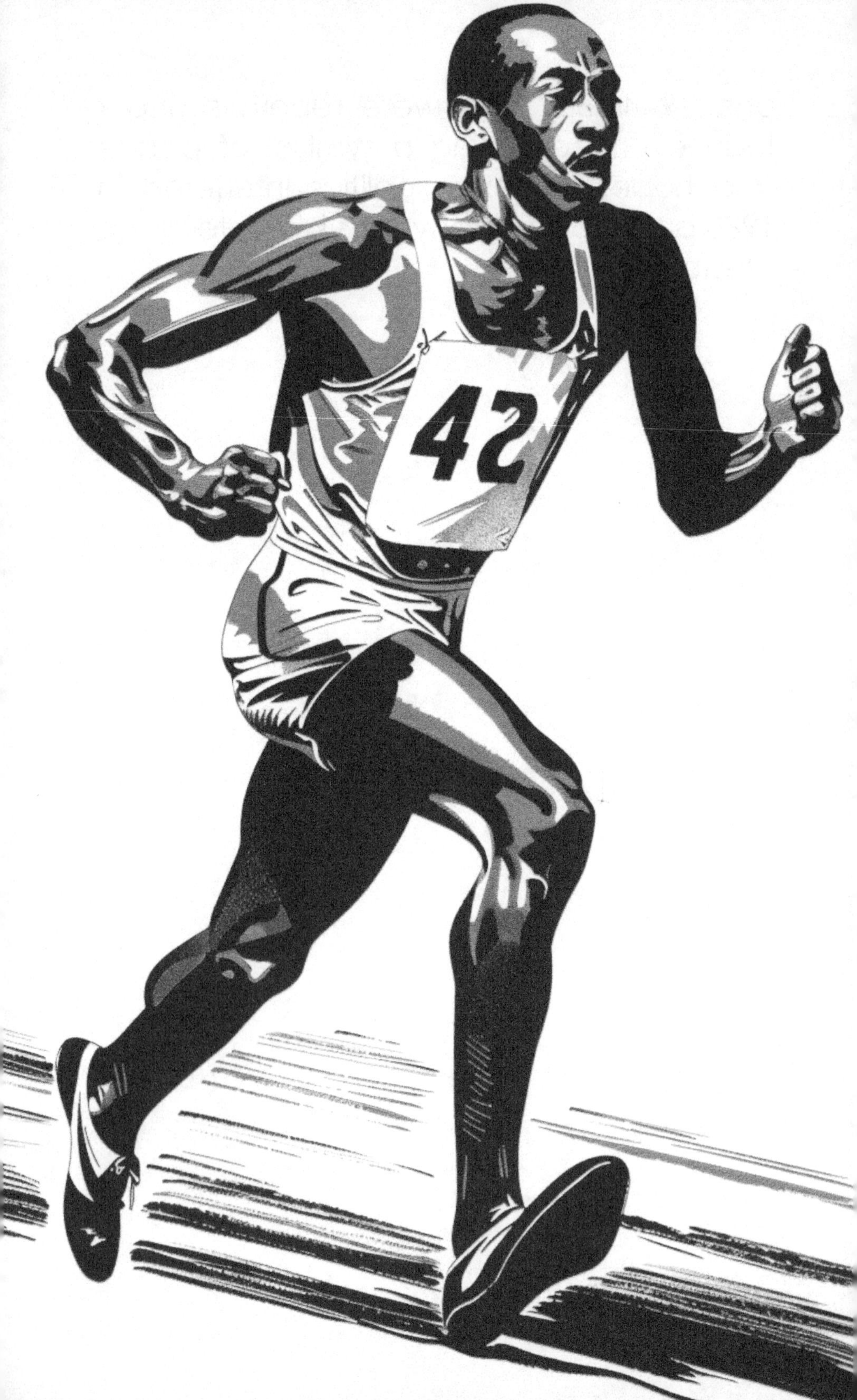
42

Legends of the Olympic Games

Jesse Owens: The Black Lightning Who Defied Hitler

Imagine a dark time where hatred and discrimination reigned. In Nazi Germany in 1936, the Olympic Games were held under the shadow of Hitler's racist ideology. But amidst this hostile environment, a young African American named Jesse Owens was about to challenge the world with his talent and determination.

Born in Alabama, United States, Owens was a prodigy in athletics. From a young age, he demonstrated an incredible ability to run, jump, and throw, breaking records and leaving everyone astonished. At 23, he arrived in Berlin with a dream: to prove that skin color does not define a person.

And he certainly achieved it. Owens dazzled the world with his speed and power, winning four gold medals in the 100 meters, 200 meters, long jump, and 4x100 meter relay events. His victories were a blow to the

Nazi regime, which had hoped to use the Games to promote their supremacist ideology.

The crowd, initially hostile towards Owens, was stunned by his talent and sportsmanship. In the end, they couldn't help but applaud and celebrate his achievements. During the long jump award ceremony, Owens received congratulations from Hitler himself, who was forced to acknowledge his talent despite his racist beliefs. Owens, with his characteristic humility, simply greeted the Nazi leader with a courteous gesture.

Owens became a symbol of hope for oppressed people around the world, demonstrating that sports can unite people and overcome the barriers of hatred.

Hedwig Ballin: The Gymnast Who Defied the Nazi Regime

Hedwig was an exceptional gymnast. From a young age, she demonstrated incredible skill and passion for the sport, training hard to achieve excellence. But her path was not easy. As a Jewish woman, she faced discrimination and hostility in Nazi Germany.

Despite the difficulties, Hedwig did not give up. With a heart full of courage, she decided to compete in the 1936 Berlin Olympic Games, challenging the Nazi regime and defending her right to participate in the sport she loved.

On the field, Hedwig captivated the audience with her elegance, precision, and determination. Her movements were flawless, full of grace and strength. Despite the hostile environment, her talent and unwavering spirit shone brightly.

Hedwig won a silver medal in the team competition, an achievement that filled her with pride and hope. During the award ceremony, Hedwig refused to give the Nazi salute when receiving her silver medal. This gesture of defiance was an act of bravery that made her an even more powerful symbol of resistance against the Nazi regime.

After the Olympic Games, Hedwig emigrated to the United States, where she continued competing and teaching gymnastics. Her story became an icon of resistance against discrimination and oppression, inspiring generations to fight for their dreams and defend their rights.

Nadia Comăneci: The "Golden Girl" Who Achieved Perfection

Montreal 1976. The world of gymnastics was about to witness a magical moment, a turning point in the sport. The protagonist of this historic milestone: a young Romanian gymnast named Nadia Comăneci, who at just 14 years old achieved perfection and left the audience in awe.

From a young age, Nadia demonstrated exceptional talent, combining grace, strength, and control in every movement. Her passion for gymnastics was evident, and her dedication and hard work made her a promising athlete.

On that July night in Montreal, Nadia took to the floor with a radiant smile and unbreakable determination. Her routine was an ode to perfection: impeccable jumps, fluid pirouettes, and flawless landings. The audience watched mesmerized, captivated by the magic emanating from the young gymnast.

At the end of her routine, a number appeared that had never been seen in the history of gymnastics: a perfect 10. (The electronic scoreboard at the time was not programmed to display a 10, so a makeshift card with the perfect score was used to honor Nadia's achievement).

A stunned silence fell over the arena, followed by an explosion of applause and cheers that echoed throughout the stadium. Nadia had achieved the impossible; she had conquered perfection.

Carl Lewis: The King of Speed

Los Angeles 1984. The Olympic Stadium crackles with the energy of a legendary sprinter: Carl Lewis. With a piercing gaze and unwavering determination, Lewis prepares to conquer the track, making it clear that this will be his stage of glory.

Over the course of those Olympic Games, Lewis cemented himself as the undisputed king of speed. With refined technique and explosive power, he dominated the 100 meters, 200 meters, long jump, and 4x100 meter relay, winning four gold medals.

Throughout his athletic career, Carl Lewis amassed a total of 10 Olympic gold medals, becoming one of the most decorated athletes in history. His dominance in the sprint and long jump events earned him the nickname "The Son of Wind," a metaphor that perfectly captures his incredible talent and speed.

Michael Jordan: The Global Icon Who Transcended the Sport

At the tender age of 21, basketball player Michael Jordan was preparing to make his debut at the 1984 Los Angeles Olympics, an opportunity that would catapult him to worldwide fame and establish him as a global icon.

From the moment he stepped onto the Olympic court, Jordan showcased his unparalleled talent. With every move, every jump, and every dunk, he captivated the audience with his spectacularity and mastery of the game. His acrobatic style and ability to defy gravity made him a unique and unrepeatable figure, capturing the attention of basketball fans around the world.

During his participation in the Los Angeles

Olympics, Michael Jordan averaged 19.3 points per game, leading the United States team to the gold medal. Additionally, his spectacular dunk over German defender Uwe Blab in the final became one of the most iconic images in the history of Olympic basketball.

But Jordan didn't just win over the audience with his on-court talent. His charisma and personal magnetism made him a media figure of epic proportions. His contagious smile, positive attitude, and unmistakable style made him a pop culture icon, captivating people of all ages and backgrounds.

Usain Bolt: The Human Lightning Bolt Who Redefined Speed

A name that resonates powerfully in the history of athletics, synonymous with speed, power, and an infectious smile that lit up the tracks. Born in Trelawny, Jamaica in 1986, Bolt became a living legend, defying human limits and redefining what was considered possible in the world of sport.

From an early age, Bolt displayed exceptional talent for speed. At the age of 12, he was already running the 100 meters in under 12 seconds, a feat that positioned him as a rising star in Jamaican athletics. His passion for the sport and his dedication to training made him a force to be reckoned with on the tracks.

In 2008, the world witnessed the birth of a legend at the Beijing Olympics. Bolt swept the 100 and 200-meter races, breaking world records and leaving his rivals no chance of competing. His dominance of the tracks was absolute, and his unique style, characterized by his explosive acceleration and triumphant smile, made him a global icon.

At the 2012 London Olympics, Bolt repeated his feat, becoming the first man in history to win gold medals in the 100 meters, 200 meters, and 4x100 meter relay in two consecutive Olympics. His historic triple-triple cemented his status as the most dominant sprinter of all time, an athlete who redefined the limits of human speed. Bolt reached a top speed of 44.72 kilometers per hour in the

100 meters, a speed comparable to that of a cheetah.

Bolt not only impressed with his speed but also with his charismatic personality and his ability to connect with the public. His infectious smile, his on-track dances, and his relaxed attitude made him one of the most beloved athletes in the world, inspiring millions of people to pursue their dreams with passion and determination.

Abebe Bikila: The Barefoot Marathon Legend

Abebe Bikila, an Ethiopian marathoner, etched his name in the annals of sporting history with his extraordinary feats, including winning the gold medal in the marathon at the 1960 Rome Olympics while running barefoot.

Born in Jato, Ethiopia in 1932, Bikila displayed exceptional aptitude for athletics from a young age, training barefoot in the mountains, a common practice in his community. His feet, hardened and calloused, were perfectly adapted to the rugged terrain.

In 1952, Bikila embarked on his international competitive journey, quickly establishing himself as a force to be reckoned with in the world of running. He claimed numerous victories in his home country and abroad, including the African Marathon Championships in 1958.

At the 1960 Rome Olympics, Bikila entered the marathon. However, upon arriving at the Olympic Village, he faced a dilemma: he couldn't find shoes that fit him properly. With the race approaching rapidly, he made a bold decision – he would run barefoot, just as he had trained.

Despite the doubts and criticisms of some, Bikila took to the track with unwavering determination. His race was nothing short of impeccable. Leading from the start, he set a steady pace that no one could match. Finally, he crossed

the finish line in first place, clocking in at 2 hours, 15 minutes, and 16 seconds. This remarkable feat shattered the world record and made him the first African athlete to clinch a gold medal in a distance event.

In 1964, Bikila repeated his triumph at the

Tokyo Olympics, this time running with shoes. He further cemented his dominance by winning the World Marathon Championships in 1965.

Simone Biles: The Gymnastics Artist

Simone Biles, an American gymnast, has revolutionized the sport with her exceptional talent, charisma, and courage. Her name is etched in history as one of the most successful gymnasts of all time, with a record-breaking 32 medals, including 19 gold at world championships and the Olympics.

Simone Biles was born in 1997 in Columbus, Ohio. From a young age, she displayed a remarkable aptitude for gymnastics. At the age of 6, she began training at the Karolyi Gymnastics Training Center, where she developed into an exceptional athlete under the guidance of Béla and Márta Károlyi.

Her international debut came in 2013, at the tender age of 16. Since then, Biles has been unstoppable, dominating competitions and shattering records one after another.

Biles has claimed 4 individual gold medals and 4 team gold medals at the 2016 Rio Olympics and the 2020 Tokyo Olympics.

She has been a world champion on 15 occasions, including 6 times in the all-around category.

Biles has received numerous accolades, including the Laureus World Sports Award for Sportswoman of the Year and the ESPY Award for Best Female Athlete.

In 2021, during the Tokyo Olympics, Biles made the courageous decision to withdraw from some competitions due to mental health concerns. Her decision was met with worldwide applause and sparked an important conversation about mental health in sports.

Eliud Kipchoge: The Marathon King Who Rewrites History

Eliud Kipchoge, known as "The Marathon King," has not only gone down in history as one of the best runners of all time, but he has rewritten it with every stride. His dominance in the 42.195-kilometer distance is almost absolute: he has won all but one of the marathons he has competed in, including Olympic gold medals in Rio 2016 and Tokyo 2020, and eight victories in the prestigious Marathon Majors of London, Chicago, and Berlin. But his legacy goes beyond victories. Kipchoge holds the official world record for the marathon with a blistering time of 2:01:39, set at the 2018 Berlin Marathon. This mark represents a reduction of one minute and 18 seconds from the previous record, demonstrating his ability to push the limits of human performance.

Born in the Kenyan district of Nandi, Kipchoge has been competing at the highest level since 2002. His beginnings were marked by the 5000 meters, where he achieved great success, such as bronze at the 2004 Athens Olympics and silver at Beijing 2008. However, it was in the marathon that Kipchoge found his true dimension, becoming a living legend of athletics.

Bob Beamon's Stratospheric Leap

Mexico City 1968 Olympics. A stadium on the edge of its seat. Bob Beamon sprints, takes off, and defies gravity. 8.90 meters. The new world record shattering the previous one by 55 cm. Tears, jubilation, a historic milestone. Unbeaten for 23 years. A leap into the unknown, a symbol of human limits. Beamon's mark was so impressive that the measuring devices of the time were not prepared to record it. They had to improvise a new scale to measure his feat!

Derek Redmond: The Father Who Ran with His Injured Son

Derek Redmond was a 400-meter runner with high aspirations. In 1992, he arrived in Barcelona as one of the medal favorites. However, fate had another plan for him. In the semifinals, Redmond suffered a severe hamstring injury that sent him crashing to the ground. His dream of a medal seemed to vanish.

In that moment of despair, the figure of John Redmond, Derek's father, became the light that illuminated the darkness. Regardless of the rules or protocols, John jumped over the security barriers and rushed to his son on the track.

With tears in his eyes and pain etched on his face, Derek refused to give up. Leaning on his father's shoulder, he completed the lap of the track, limping but with his head held high. The crowd rose to their feet, moved by this act of love and determination.

Oleksandr Usyk: Ukrainian Boxing Hero and Undisputed Champion

Oleksandr Usyk is a Ukrainian boxer who has captured the hearts of his country and the world with his talent, determination, and unwavering spirit. His amateur career was marked by victories in various championships, including the world championship in 2011 and the gold medal at the 2012 London Olympics. In 2013, he made the leap to professional boxing and signed a contract with K2 Promotions. His first professional fight was a resounding success, kicking off a string of victories that propelled him to the top of the sport.

What makes Oleksandr Usyk special is his unique and unmatched style in the ring. His technical mastery, strategic thinking, and ability to adapt to any opponent make him an exceptional boxer. Usyk has not only won numerous titles but has also become a source of inspiration for young boxers around the world.

On May 18, 2024, Oleksandr Usyk retained his undisputed heavyweight title in an exciting bout against Tyson Fury. In a fight full of tension and strategy, Usyk once again demonstrated his technical and tactical superiority, overcoming a formidable opponent and solidifying his place as one of the greatest boxers of all time. This victory was not only a historic sporting achievement but also a symbol of hope and pride for the Ukrainian people amidst a complex historical context.

Ibtihaj Muhammad: The Fencer Who Broke Barriers with Her Hijab

At the 2016 Rio Olympic Games, Ibtihaj Muhammad became the first Muslim American woman to compete in fencing while wearing a hijab. Her participation challenged stereotypes and paved the way for other athletes with similar beliefs to compete at the highest level in sports.

Muhammad won a bronze medal in team sabre, inspiring women around the world to pursue their dreams regardless of cultural or religious differences.

Félix Sánchez: Overcoming Poverty and Tragedy to Achieve Olympic Glory

Félix Sánchez, a Dominican athlete, was born into poverty and violence in a marginalized neighborhood in the Dominican Republic. Despite these challenges, he found athletics as a path to a better life.

At the 2004 Athens Olympics, Sánchez achieved the gold medal in the 400-meter hurdles, becoming the first Dominican athlete to reach Olympic glory. His victory was a symbol of hope and overcoming adversity for his country and a message that dreams can come true with effort and determination.

John Stephen Akhwari: The

Marathon of Willpower

At the 1956 Melbourne Olympics, Tanzanian marathoner John Stephen Akhwari staggered and bloodied to the finish line. Around the 30-kilometer mark, Akhwari had taken a nasty fall. He crumpled to the ground, injuring his legs and knee. The pain was excruciating, and many thought his race was over.

Despite the intense pain, Akhwari refused to give up. He got back up and continued the race, determined to finish what he had started. The crowd erupted in cheers as they saw him limping in, the Tanzanian flag held high. Some spectators even believed he was dead and that his ghost was completing the race.

Although he did not win a medal, Akhwari had completed the race and demonstrated a spirit of perseverance and determination that made him a hero to his country and the world.

Sergey Bubka: The Pole Vault King and His Incredible Records

Sergey Bubka was a Ukrainian athlete who dominated pole vaulting during his career, breaking the men's world record an astonishing 35 times. His dominance was such that he only lost his outdoor record once, and he regained it on his next attempt on the same runway! Bubka excelled not only outdoors but also indoors, where he also broke the world record 18 times.

Despite his immense talent, Bubka did not have the best of luck at the Olympics. He competed in four editions but only managed to win one gold medal in Seoul 1988. On two other occasions, he was forced to withdraw due to injuries.

Without a doubt, Bubka was an exceptional athlete who left an indelible mark on the history of pole vaulting. His name remains synonymous with dominance, tenacity, and passion for the sport.

The Refugee Olympic Team: A Story of Hope and Perseverance

In the world of sports, the Refugee Olympic Team (EOR) has emerged as a symbol of hope, perseverance, and the triumph of the human spirit in the face of adversity. Its story, which began in 2016, is filled with moving moments and inspiring lessons.

The creation of the EOR took root in 2015 amidst an unprecedented global refugee crisis. The International Olympic Committee (IOC), moved by the plight of millions of people displaced by war and violence, made the decision to provide them with an opportunity to compete in the Olympics as a symbol of unity and hope.

In 2016, during the Rio de Janeiro Olympics, the EOR made its official debut. A group of 10 athletes from Syria, South Sudan, Congo, Ethiopia, and Iran formed the team, competing in disciplines such as athletics, swimming, and judo.

Their participation transcended the realm of sport, capturing the world's attention and

sending a powerful message of solidarity and inclusion. The EOR athletes did not just compete for medals; they represented the strength and resilience of millions of refugees seeking a better future.

In 2021, at the Tokyo Olympics, the EOR participated once again, this time with a team of 29 athletes from 12 countries. Among them was Yusra Mardini, the Syrian swimmer who escaped her country on an inflatable raft and then went on to help save other refugees. These athletes have overcome wars, persecutions, and dangerous journeys, but their passion for sport and their determination to succeed have taken them to the top of the Olympic stage.

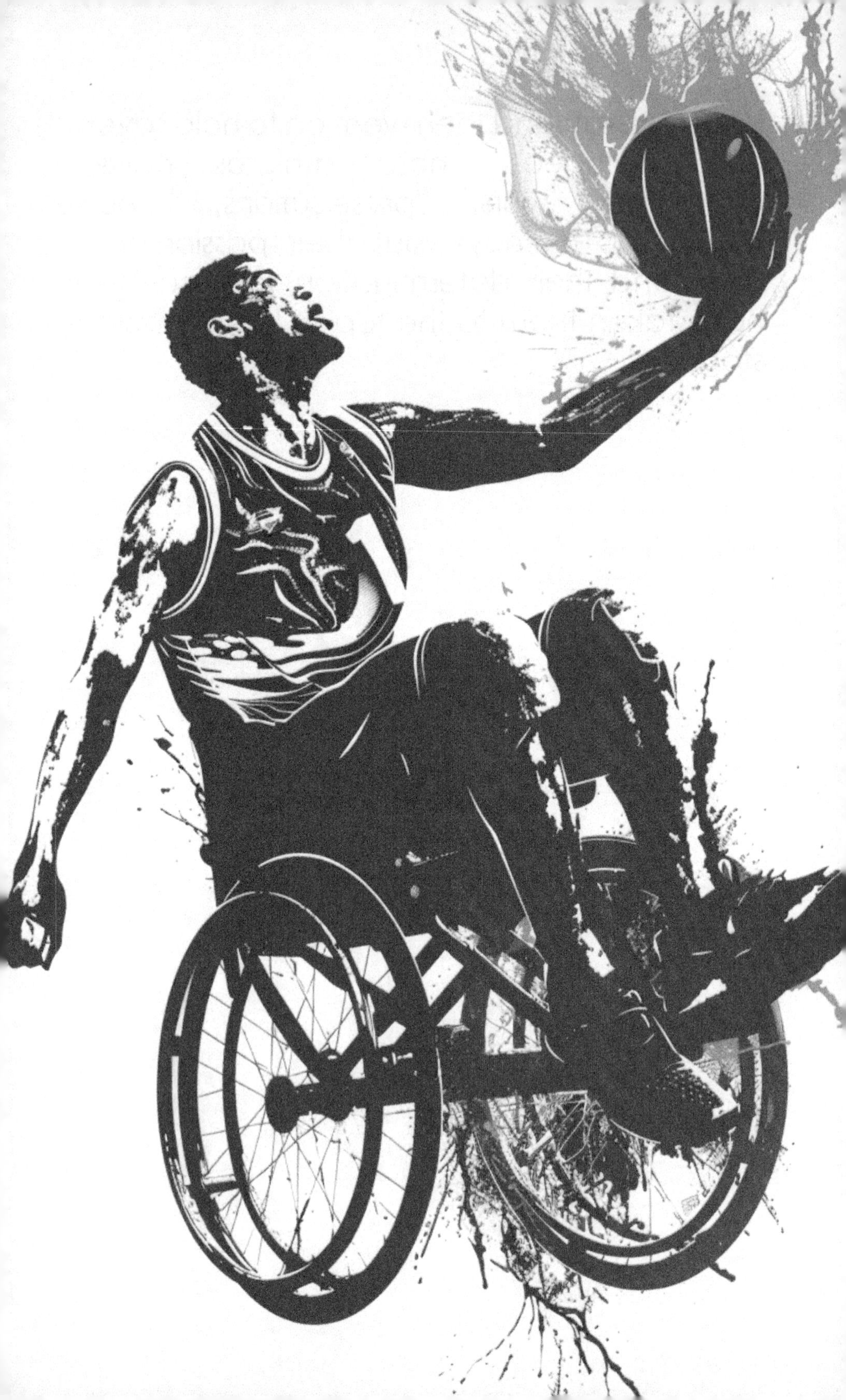

Paralympic Games

Imagine a sporting competition where athletes with physical disabilities compete at the highest level. This is the Paralympic Games! Born from the idea of Ludwig Guttmann, a doctor who believed in the power of sport for rehabilitation, these games have grown into a global event that inspires and excites.

Skiing with One Leg: Defying Gravity!

Imagine gliding down the snow at full speed with only one leg to maintain balance. That's what para-alpine skiers do at the Paralympic Games! An inspiring example is Michael Brügger from Switzerland, who despite losing his right leg in a motorcycle accident, has won several gold medals in these competitions.

Wheelchair Basketball: An Unstoppable Team!

The United States wheelchair basketball team is a legend. They have won an incredible 25 gold medals at the Paralympic Games, including the last 16 consecutive ones! Their dominance is a testament to their teamwork, dedication, and exceptional talent.

Snowboarding: Overcoming Adversity on the Snow!

Chinese snowboarder Kaiyang Liu lost his leg at the young age of five. However, that didn't stop him from pursuing his passion for this sport. At the Beijing 2022 Paralympic Games, Liu fulfilled his dream of representing his country in the competition, a true story of overcoming adversity!

Archers Without Arms: Aiming for Glory!

Matt Stutzman was born without arms, but that didn't stop him from becoming an elite archer. At the age of 8, he discovered his passion for this sport, and with a specially adapted bow and arrows, began practicing. His talent and dedication led him to the London 2012 Paralympic Games, where he won a silver medal. In 2014, Stutzman made history by becoming the first armless archer to compete in a professional tournament. He has since won numerous championships and set world records.

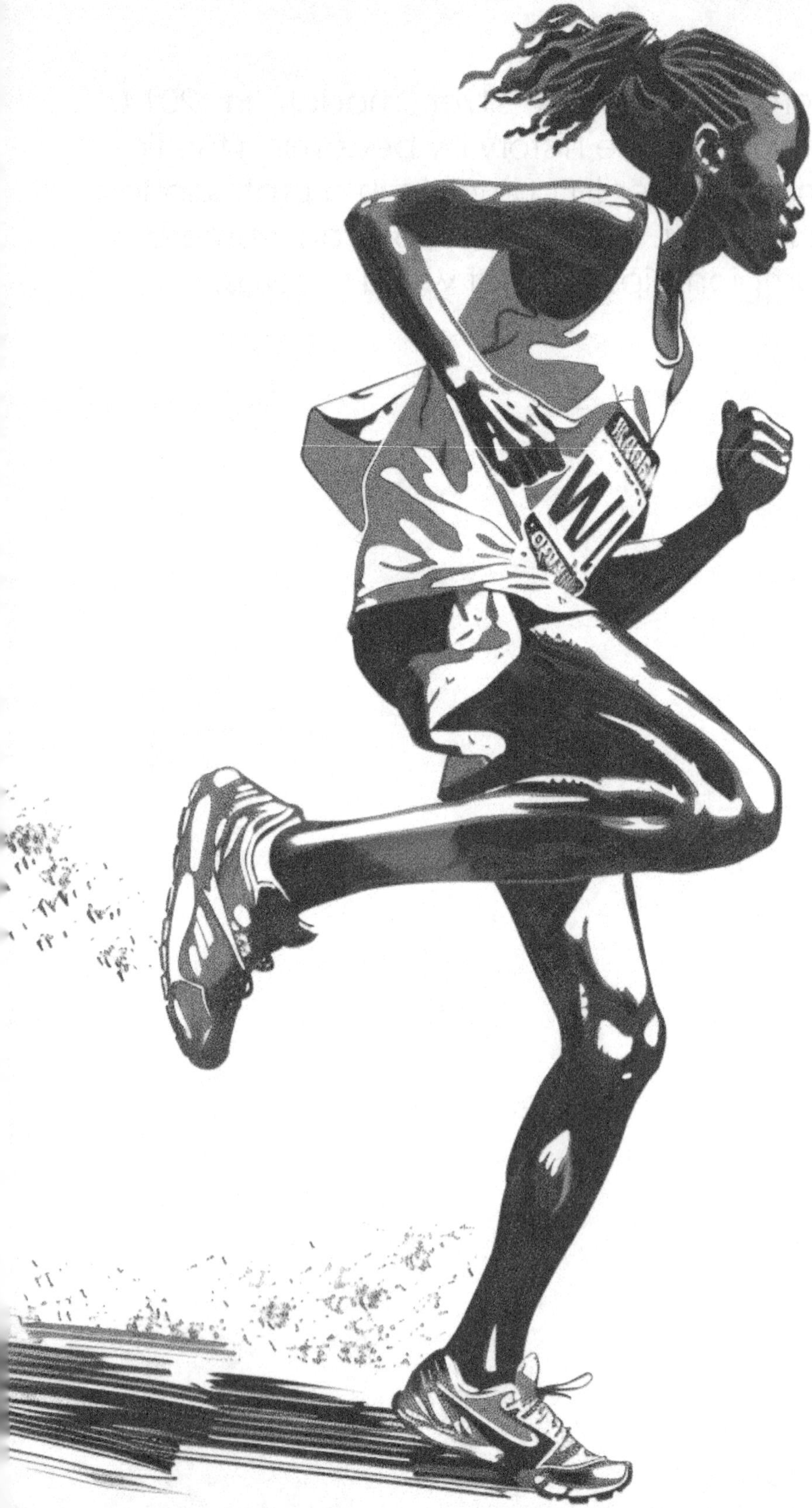

Women in the Olympic Games

Charlotte Cooper: The First Female Olympic Champion

In the world of sports, gender equality has been a constant battle. At the beginning of the 20th century, women were excluded from most athletic competitions. However, one woman broke barriers and became an icon: Charlotte Cooper.

At the age of 23 in 1893, Charlotte Cooper had already won her first singles title at the Ilkley Club. Her passion for tennis led her to join the Ealing Lawn Tennis Club, where she honed her skills and began to achieve success.

In 1900, Cooper participated in the Paris Olympics, the first to allow female participation. After a hard road, she reached the women's singles final and became the first woman to win an Olympic title.

Throughout her career, Cooper

participated in 21 Wimbledon Championships, playing a total of 11 finals. Her last major triumph came in 1908 when she won the Wimbledon title at the age of 37 years and 282 days, a record that still stands today.

Sarah Attar: Breaking Barriers and Inspiring Change

Sarah Attar is a Saudi-American athlete who competed in the London 2012 and Rio 2016 Olympics, making history as one of the first women to represent Saudi Arabia in Olympic competition.

Born in California, USA, Attar grew up with a passion for athletics. However, her Olympic dreams were challenged by the restrictions imposed on women in Saudi Arabia, her home country. Despite the difficulties, Attar persevered, training hard and competing in international events under the American flag.

In 2012, Attar made a major breakthrough by being selected to represent Saudi Arabia at the London Olympics. However, to compete, she had to overcome an additional challenge: obtaining permission from her father and the Saudi Olympic Committee. Additionally, dress regulations required her to compete in a hijab and a shirt that covered most of her body.

Attar not only competed in London 2012, but she also returned to the track at the Rio 2016 Olympics, demonstrating her determination and resilience.

Allison Felix: A Champion on and off the Track

American sprinter Allison Felix holds the title

of the most decorated athlete in her country's history, with 11 Olympic medals, 6 of them gold. A year after the birth of her daughter in 2019, Felix returned to the track and captured two gold medals at the World Athletics Championships. Felix shines not only on the track but also off it. She spoke out against the pay discrimination she experienced at Nike, her sponsor, due to her pregnancy. She advocates for gender equality and support for athlete mothers, demonstrating that motherhood is not an obstacle to sporting success.

Paula Radcliffe: Balancing Motherhood and Elite Athletics

In 2003, Radcliffe set a world record of 2:15:25 in the London Marathon, a mark that stood for 16 years. A mother of two young children at the time of her feat, Radcliffe showed that balancing family life with high-level sport is possible. Throughout her career, Radcliffe faced several injuries, but her determination and mental strength propelled her to overcome them and reach the pinnacle of athletics.

Tegla Loroupe: A Pioneer for African Women in Running

In 1994, Loroupe became the first African woman to win a marathon, the Boston World Marathon Majors. Loroupe is not only an elite runner but also a mother of five children. Her story demonstrates that motherhood does not have to limit one's sporting dreams. Loroupe is committed to promoting sport and education in Africa, especially for girls and women.

Jessica Ennis-Hill: A Comeback After Motherhood

Jessica Ennis-Hill is one of the most decorated athletes in the UK, with two Olympic gold medals and three world titles in heptathlon. In 2016, Ennis-Hill gave birth to her son and returned to competition a year later, winning the silver medal at the 2016 Rio Olympics.

Serena Williams: A Tennis Icon and Mother

And let's not forget Serena Williams, who after the birth of her daughter in 2017, continued to dominate the world of tennis.

These women are inspiring examples that demonstrate that motherhood can be a source of strength, not an end to a sporting career.

Lida Peyton Pollock: The Oldest Gold Medalist in History

Do you think 63 is too old to compete in the Olympics? Well, Lida Peyton Pollock would prove you wrong! This incredible American archer not only participated in the 1904 Olympics at the age of 63 but also won the team gold medal alongside her teammates William Henry Thompson and William J. Lucas.

Unlike most Olympic athletes, Lida was not a professional archer. In fact, she was a physical education teacher and the principal of a girls' school. However, her passion for the sport was undeniable. Lida began practicing archery at the age of 40 and quickly became an expert. Her talent and dedication led her to compete in the 1904 St. Louis Olympics, where she made history by becoming the oldest woman to win a gold medal.

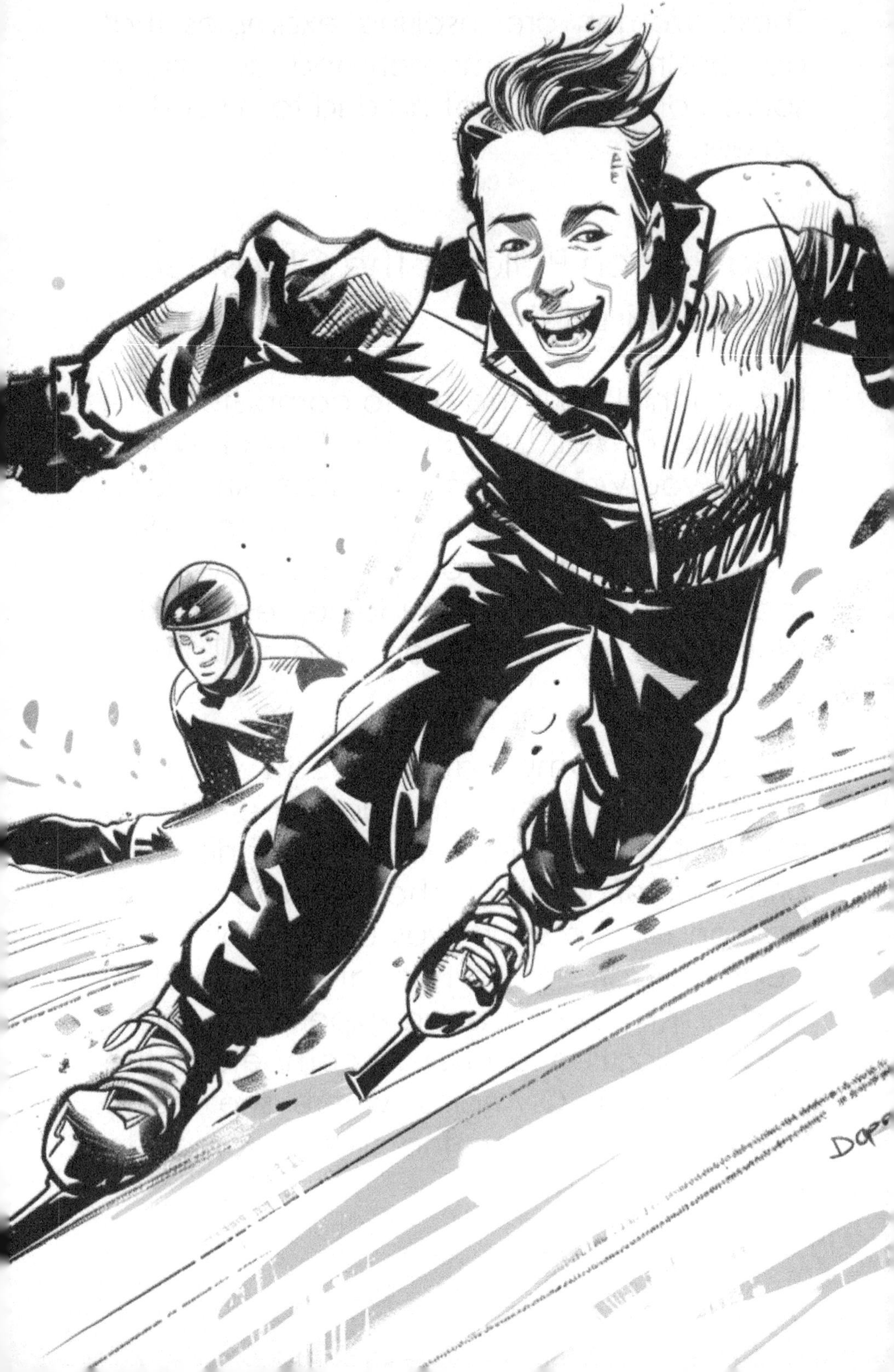

The First Winter Olympics

Imagine competing on snow and ice? In 1924, on the snowy slopes of the French Alps, it became a reality: the first Winter Olympics!

The idea of a Winter Olympics was born in 1894, but it was not until 1921 that its creation was official. Chamonix, with its imposing mountains and experience in winter events, was chosen as the ideal venue.

From January 25 to February 5, 1924, 258 athletes from 28 countries competed in 9 sports and 16 disciplines. These included alpine and Nordic skiing, figure skating, bobsleigh, and curling.

Sonja Henie, a young Norwegian woman of only 15 years old, captivated the audience with her elegant figure skating, winning the first gold medal in this discipline.

Clas Thunberg, an unstoppable Finn, became a legend by winning five gold medals in speed skating.

Charles Jewtraw from the United States was crowned the first Olympic champion in the 500 meters speed skating.

Despite the difficulties of the time, the Chamonix Games were a resounding success. They attracted thousands of spectators and showed the world the potential and passion for winter sports.

Here are some additional details about the Chamonix 1924 Winter Olympics:

- The opening ceremony took place on January 25, 1924, at the Olympic Stadium in Chamonix.

- The closing ceremony took place on February 5, 1924, at the same venue.

- The Olympic flame was lit for the first time at these Games.

- The Olympic oath was taken for the first time at these Games.

- The mascot for the Games was a Chamois, a type of goat that is native to the Alps.

The Chamonix 1924 Winter Olympics were a pivotal moment in the history of winter sports. They helped to popularize winter sports around the world and paved the way for the future Winter Olympics.

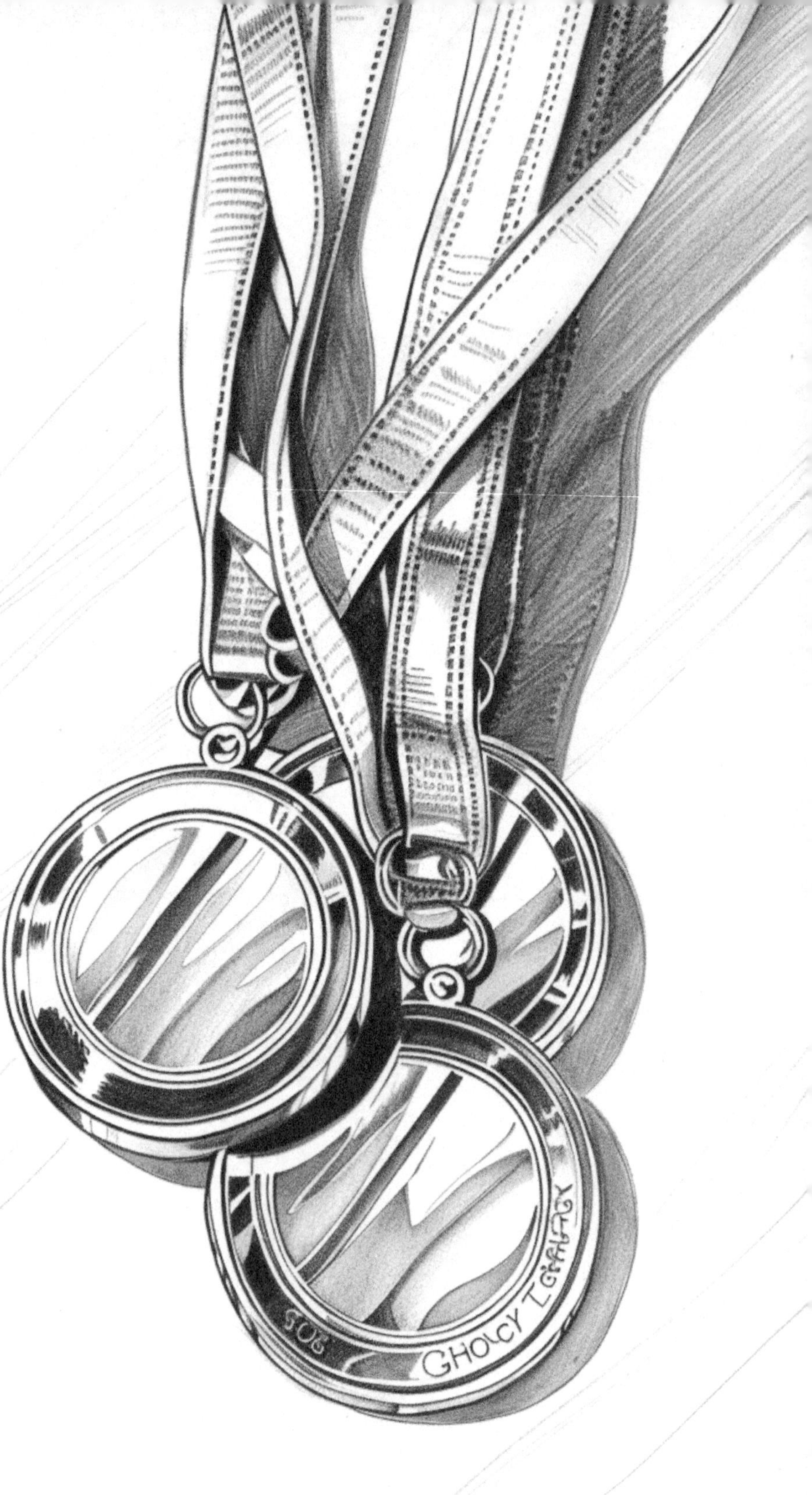

Symbolism of Medals

Imagine standing on the top of the podium, the world watching, a gold medal hanging around your neck. It's more than just a prize; it's a symbol of your hard work, dedication, and the dream fulfilled of becoming an Olympic champion. But did you know that these medals that represent sporting glory hide some secrets?

Olympic medals are made of a mixture of metals, although they do contain a percentage of gold (around 6%). Silver and bronze medals are also made of special alloys.

Each edition of the Olympic Games has its own medal design, but some key elements remain: the Games logo and the year on the obverse and the International Olympic Committee design on the reverse.

Medals aren't made just anywhere. Each host city chooses a local company with experience in jewelry or metalworking to create these unique pieces.

Gold, silver, and bronze represent the top three places in each competition. But the reverse design can go further, including elements of the host country or Olympic culture.

Some athletes auction their medals or donate them to charities. Others become family heirlooms or museum pieces.

Throughout history, some medals have attracted attention for their originality, creativity, and even a touch of humor bordering on what some might consider "funny."

- Barcelona 1992: A map of the Iberian Peninsula on the reverse, which some considered too abstract.

- Sydney 2000: A representation of an Aboriginal corroboree, which some found too culturally specific.

- London 2012: An abstract design inspired by the River Thames, which some considered too modern.

- Paris 2024: A mystery yet to be discovered. The Paris medals have not yet been revealed, but anticipation is already running high. They are expected to incorporate elements that represent the city's culture and history, such as the Eiffel Tower or the Seine River.

Behind each Olympic medal is a story of hard work, dedication, and exceptional talent. Some athletes have managed to stand out from the rest, accumulating an impressive number of medals and leaving their mark on the history of the Olympic Games.

- Michael Phelps: American swimmer with the absolute record of Olympic medals (28), 23 of them gold.

- Larisa Latynina: Soviet gymnast with the most Olympic medals for women (18), 9 of them gold.

- Carl Lewis: American sprinter with the most gold medals in men's athletics (9).

- The oldest athlete to win a gold was Tom Longboat (athletics) at the age of 40 in 1900.

- The youngest athlete to win a silver was Inge Heitmann (swimming) at the age of 13 in 1936.

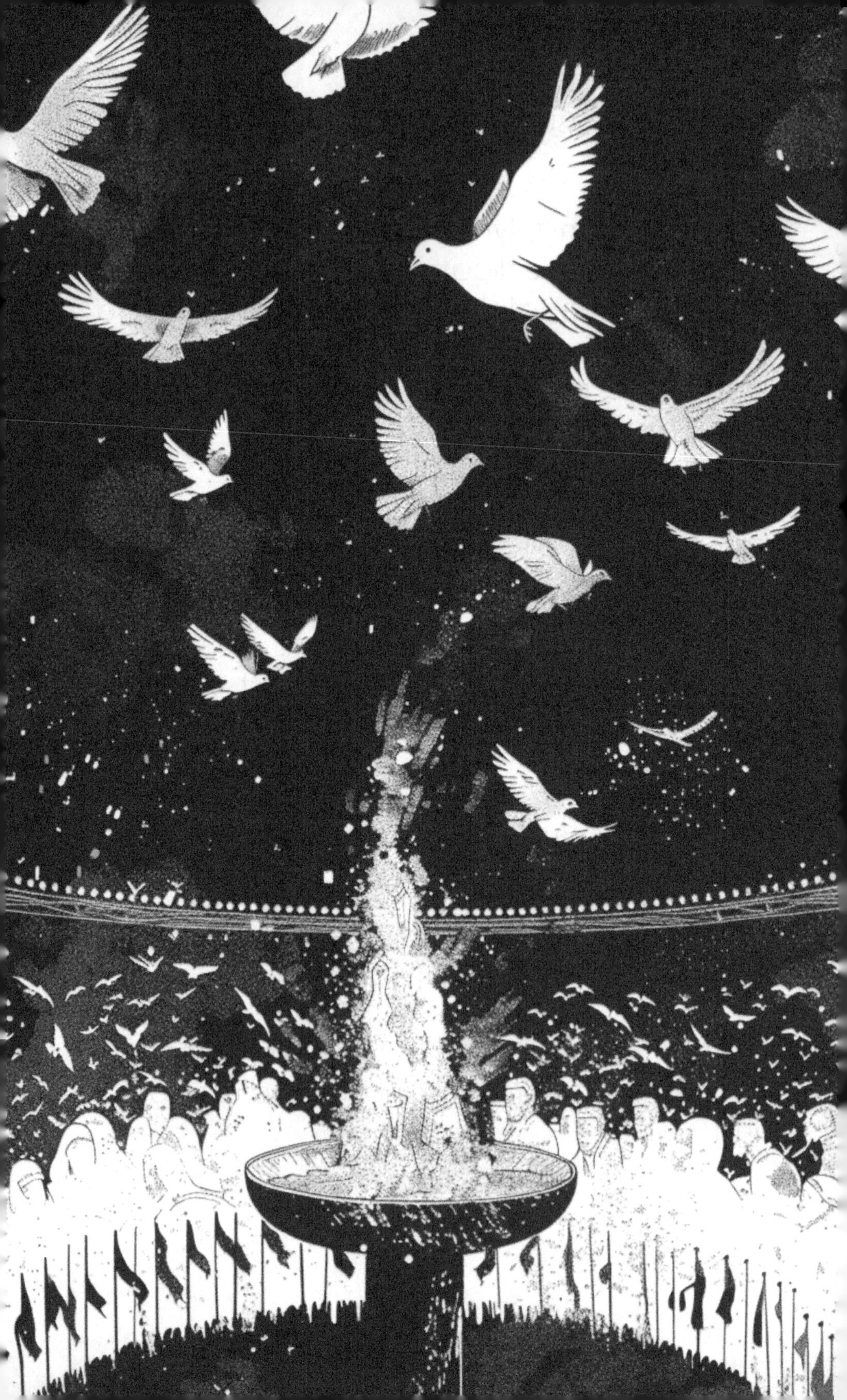

Opening Ceremonies

The opening ceremonies of the Olympic Games are events filled with magic, symbolism, and of course, surprises! Throughout history, these celebrations have given the world unforgettable moments that have been etched into collective memory.

A Spectacle Without Precedent: In Los Angeles 1984, the opening ceremony featured the participation of more than 16,000 people, including 6,100 white doves that flew over the stadium in a spectacle never seen before.

A Journey Through Time: In Athens 2004, the Olympic Stadium was transformed into a giant pool from which the five Olympic rings emerged, marking the beginning of a journey through Greek history from ancient mythology to contemporary times.

A Message of Peace Gone Wrong: Before Seoul 1988, tradition dictated the release of doves as a symbol of world peace. However, on this occasion, a sad accident occurred when about 10 doves landed on the Olympic cauldron just at the moment it was lit, causing their deaths. As a result of this event, it was decided to put an end to this custom to prevent a similar tragedy from happening again.

A Lavish Display of Light and Color: Beijing 2008 gave us an unparalleled fireworks display lasting 29 minutes and using 14,000 tons of pyrotechnics. A display of lights and colors that illuminated the city's night sky!

Commitment to the Planet: Vancouver 2010 stood out for its commitment to the environment. The ceremony used renewable energy, recycled materials, and even a system to collect rainwater. An example of how a large-scale event can be sustainable!

Tradition, Emotion, and Humor: London 2012 gave us an unforgettable opening ceremony that combined British tradition with excitement and a touch of humor. A tribute to the country's culture was made with the appearance of Mary Poppins descending from the sky with her multicolored umbrellas. In an unexpected moment, James Bond, the world's most famous secret agent, made a surprising appearance alongside Queen Elizabeth II, parachuting from a helicopter and leaving the audience breathless. A unique moment that combined action, tradition, and a touch of British humor.

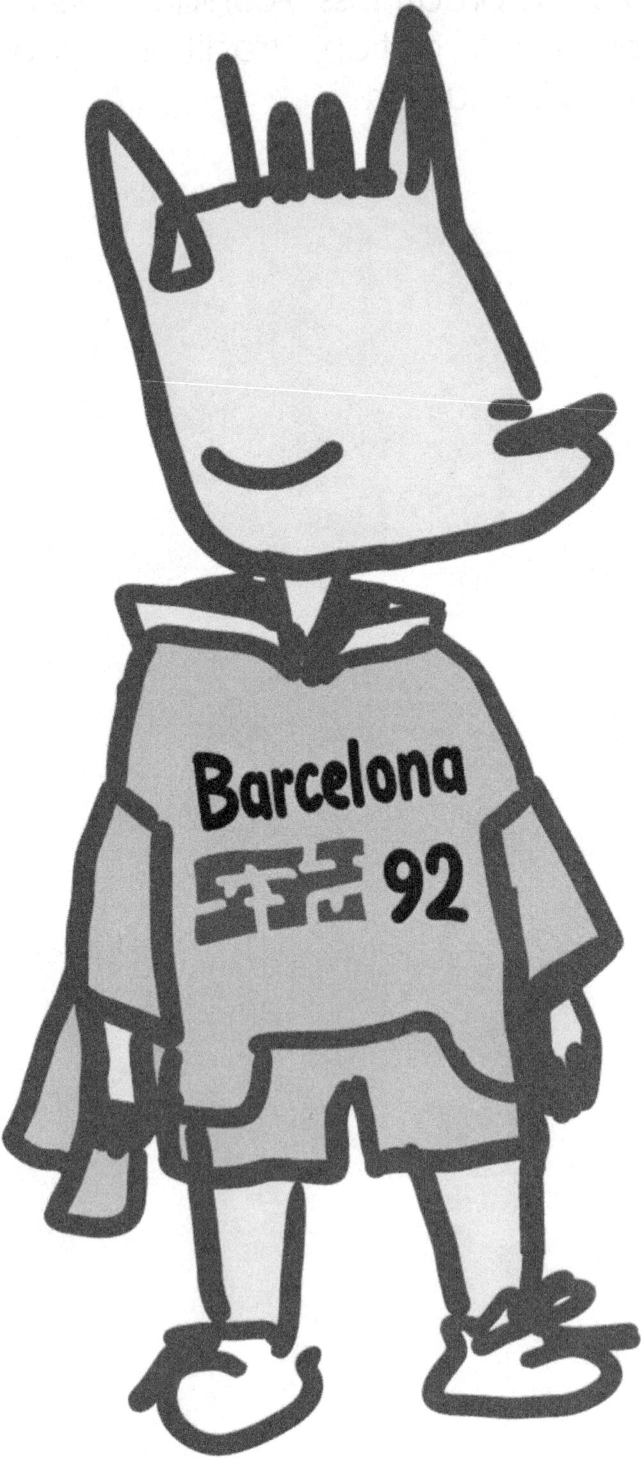
Barcelona
92

Olympic Mascots and Their Significance

Imagine a smiling brown bear, an eagle with an entrepreneurial spirit, or a duo of steel droplets with big eyes. No, they're not characters from a science fiction movie! They are some of the Olympic mascots that have accompanied the Olympic Games throughout history.

Olympic mascots are not just adorable plush figures. Each one is designed to represent the spirit of the Games, the culture of the host country, and values such as friendship, diversity, and overcoming challenges.

Misha (Moscow 1980): An adorable brown bear that symbolized the strength and resilience of the Russian people. His friendly smile and curious gaze made him one of the most beloved mascots.

Sam (Los Angeles 1984): An eagle wearing a hat, the national symbol of the United States. Sam represented the freedom, entrepreneurial spirit, and optimism of the host country.

Cobi (Barcelona 1992): A Catalan

sheepdog, a native breed of Spain. Cobi represented the friendship, loyalty, and warmth of the Spanish people.

Izzy (Atlanta 1996): A blue rock-shaped creature designed to represent diversity and inclusion. Izzy symbolized the innovative and technological spirit of the digital age.

Syd, Olly, and Millie (Sydney 2000): A platypus, a kookaburra, and an echidna, three unique and emblematic animals of Australia. The kookaburra and the platypus are two emblems of the Australian state of New South Wales, whose capital is Sydney. Syd, Millie, and Ollie represented the diversity of Australian fauna and the importance of environmental conservation.

Wenlock and Mandeville (London 2012): Two recycled steel droplets used to build the London Olympic Stadium with big bright eyes. Wenlock and Mandeville represented London's industrial transformation and the overcoming spirit of Paralympic athletes.

Vinicius (Rio de Janeiro 2016): The name pays tribute to Vinicius de Moraes, a Brazilian poet and lyricist. Vinicius is a mix of different Brazilian animals, symbolizing the joy, vibrant culture, and rich biodiversity of Brazil.

Miraitowa (Tokyo 2020): The Olympic mascot is named Miraitowa, which comes from the Japanese words "mirai" (future) and "towa" (eternity). This name was chosen to promote a future filled with eternal hope in the hearts of people around the world.

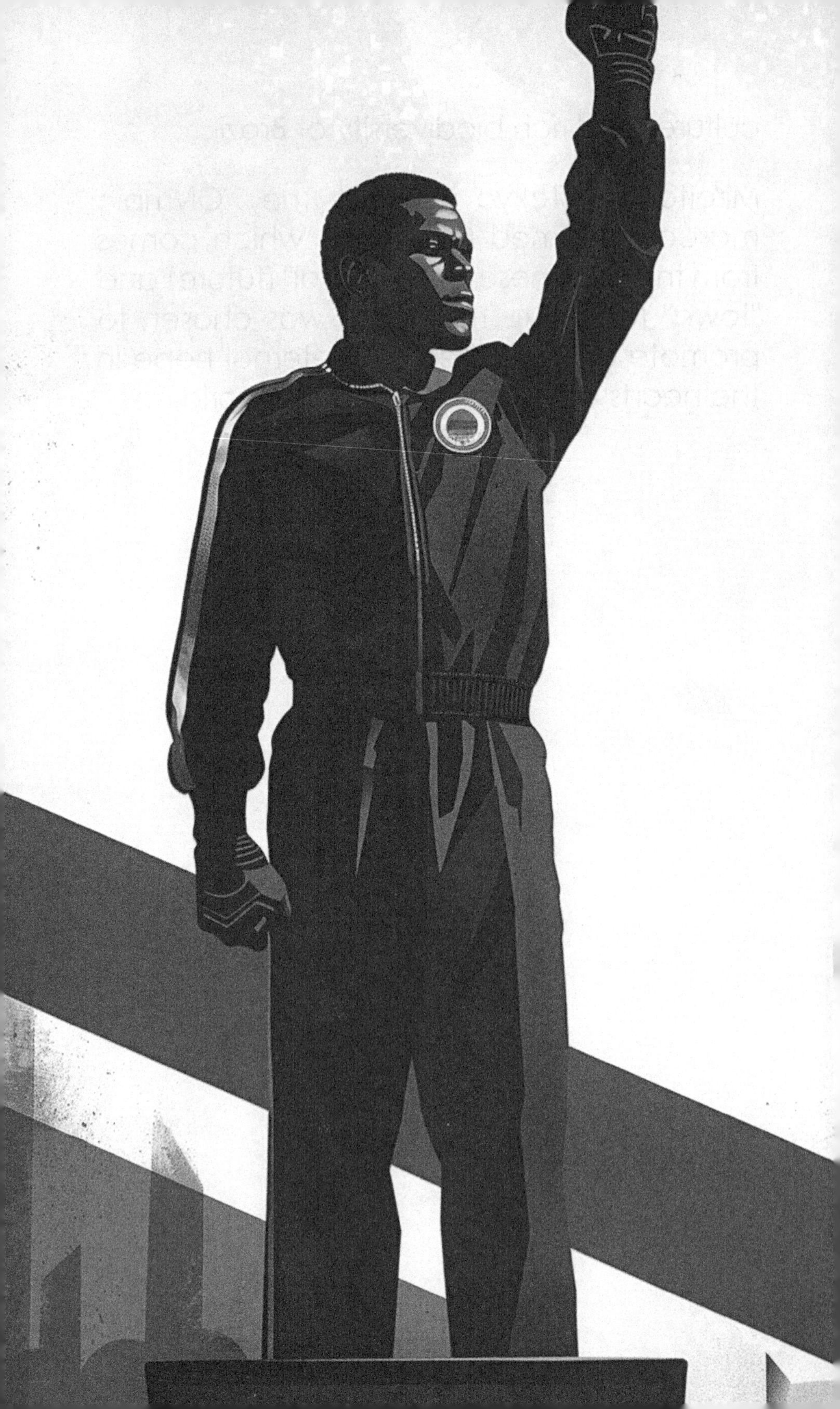

Controversy and Scandals

Imagine a place where athletes compete at the highest level, sweat on their foreheads and hearts pounding, seeking Olympic glory. But not everything is as golden as it seems. Behind the medals and records lies a world filled with controversy, scandals, and controversial decisions.

Doping: The Shadow That Clouds Glory

Doping, the practice of using banned substances to enhance performance, is like kryptonite to the Olympic spirit. Throughout history, we have seen athletes fall from grace in their pursuit of glory at any cost, consuming steroids, stimulants, or magical substances that promised to turn them into unstoppable machines. Cases like Ben Johnson in Seoul 1988 (lost his gold medal for doping) or Marion Jones in Sydney 2000 (five medals stripped for the same reason) serve as sad reminders that the shine of gold is not always real.

Political Tensions and Boycotts: When Sport Gets Tainted

The Olympic Games have also been the scene of political tensions and boycotts. In Moscow 1980, the United States and its allies did not participate in protest of the Soviet invasion of Afghanistan. And in Los Angeles 1984, the Soviet Union and its allies responded with the same gesture. These events remind us that sometimes politics interferes with sport, tarnishing the spirit of peace and unity that the Games are supposed to represent.

Stories of Cheating and Deception: When Ethics Go Missing

Olympic history is also marked by stories of cheating and deception. In 1904, American athlete Fred Lorz had the audacity to win the marathon, the toughest and most demanding event of the Games. The problem is that he did it riding in a car for most of the route. Back then, without cameras to broadcast the event, Lorz was caught after the race was over.

Chinese gymnast Dong Fangxiao falsified her age during the Sydney 2000 Games to be able to compete. Over 100 Russian athletes were banned from Rio 2016 for a state-sponsored doping scandal. For this reason, the Russian team name and flag were banned from the Tokyo 2020 Olympic Games.

Lies, Vandalism, and the Shadow of Scandal

American swimmers Ryan Lochte, Jimmy Feigen, Gunnar Bentz, and Jack Conger starred in a scandalous episode in Rio 2016. After faking an armed robbery, security cameras revealed that they vandalized a gas station while intoxicated. The United States Olympic Committee imposed sanctions: Lochte 10 months without competing; Bentz, Conger, and Feigen 4 months. This case reminds us of the responsibility that athletes must have as public figures.

Surya Bonaly's Forbidden Flip: A Tale of Defiance and Daring

At the 1998 Nagano Winter Olympics, French figure skater Surya Bonaly faced a dilemma: she couldn't perform her usual routine due to an injury. However, she didn't give up. With determination, she improvised an impressive backflip that left the audience stunned.

Unfortunately, this acrobatic move had been banned in competitions regulated by the International Skating Union since 1976. Despite its flawless execution, Bonaly was penalized for not following the established rules.

A Silent Protest: The Story of John Carlos and Tommie Smith

In the 1968 Mexico City Olympics, two African-American athletes, John Carlos and Tommie Smith, protagonized one of the most emblematic and historic moments of the Olympic Games. After winning the gold and bronze medals in the 200-meter dash, respectively, they raised their black fists on the podium as a protest against racism and racial inequality in the United States.

The 1960s in the United States were marked

by a strong civil rights movement. Numerous protests and demonstrations were organized to demand equal rights for African Americans, who faced discrimination and segregation in various aspects of life.

By winning their medals at the 1968 Mexico City Olympics, John Carlos and Tommie Smith decided to use the podium as a platform to raise awareness of the civil rights struggle. Raising their black fists, a gesture known as "Black Power," they called for unity and racial justice.

Carlos and Smith's protest generated great controversy in the Olympic community and around the world. They were expelled from the Olympic Games by the International Olympic Committee (IOC) and received numerous criticisms and threats. However, their gesture also inspired millions of people around the world and became a symbol of the fight for racial equality. Their image was etched in history as one of the most impactful moments of the Olympic Games.

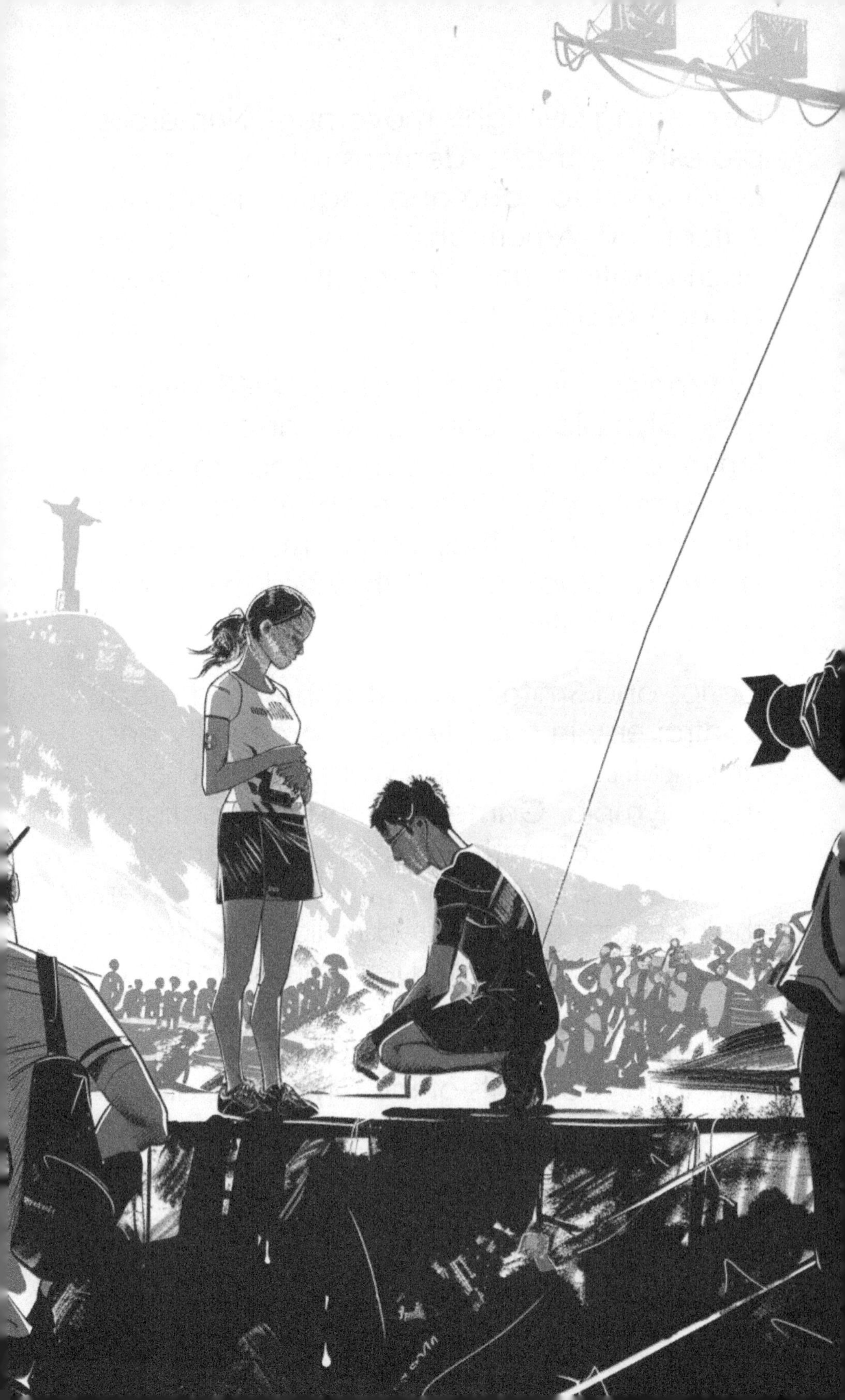

Anecdotes in the Games

The Olympic Games are not just about athletic prowess and the pursuit of gold medals; they are also about the human spirit, unexpected moments, and stories that go beyond the realm of sport. Throughout the history of the Olympics, we have witnessed acts of kindness, resilience, and humor that remind us that even in the most competitive arena, there is room for camaraderie, compassion, and a touch of the extraordinary.

Felix Carvajal: The Mailman Who Defied the Odds

In the 1904 St. Louis Olympics, Félix Carvajal, a Cuban postman, defied all odds to compete in the marathon. With limited financial resources, Carvajal embarked on a journey of over 1000 kilometers on foot to reach the competition. Despite the hardships, Carvajal led the race until a food poisoning incident and a detour relegated him to fourth place.

Carvajal's unwavering dream led him to

raise funds for his trip through donations, but in New Orleans, he lost his savings. Undeterred, he set off on foot towards St. Louis, facing harsh weather conditions and a lack of resources.

Upon reaching St. Louis, Carvajal presented himself at the starting line in his unconventional attire: postman's boots. Despite the jeers and doubts, Carvajal led the race until a food poisoning incident caused him digestive problems. A detour led him off course, but with determination, he returned to the route and finished in fourth place.

A Medal 50 Years in the Making

At the first Winter Olympics in Chamonix 1924, an unusual situation unfolded. American athlete Anders Haugen was left off the podium due to a miscalculation of scores. It wasn't until 50 years later, in 1974, that a historian reviewed the scores and discovered the injustice. Haugen, already 86 years old, finally received the bronze medal he deserved.

An Act of Kindness and Support in Nazi Germany

In 1936, in Nazi Germany, African-American athlete Jesse Owens faced a significant challenge during the long jump competition. After two unsuccessful attempts, Luz Long, a German athlete, offered him advice that allowed him to qualify for the final. Owens not only made it to the final but went on to win four gold medals. Hitler left the stadium early to avoid shaking hands with Owens at the medal ceremony.

Despite the political tension of the time, Owens received a congratulatory message from his German rival, Luz Long, in a gesture of friendship.

A Moment of Love on the Podium

In Rio de Janeiro 2016, emotions transcended the boundaries of sport. After receiving her medal on the podium, Chinese diver He Zi experienced an unforgettable moment when her boyfriend approached and proposed to her. Tears of joy and a "yes" that echoed around the world, demonstrating that love can blossom even on the Olympic stage.

An Unexpected Blunder in London 2012

Television cameras don't always capture what they should. During the London 2012 Olympics, a heptathlete was filmed in the middle of a costume change by a cameraman. The image quickly went viral, sparking a debate about athlete privacy at such events.

A Historic Mistake in the Opening Ceremony

In the same edition of London 2012, a protocol error marred the opening ceremony. The organizers, unaware of their mistake, presented the flag of South Korea instead of North Korea for the soccer players from this country. After an hour of negotiations and apologies, the error was corrected and the athletes were able to compete.

An Unconventional Ski Jumper

Eddie Edwards became a legend at the 1988 Calgary Games for his peculiar ski jumping style. Nicknamed "The Eagle" for his way of flapping his arms upon landing, Edwards was the only athlete from his country in this discipline, and despite not being the best jumper, he won the hearts of the audience for his enthusiasm and tenacity.

A Tropical Debut in the Snow

Calgary 1988 also witnessed a historic debut: the Jamaican bobsleigh team. These Caribbean athletes, with no prior experience on snow, dared to compete in a discipline dominated by European and North American countries. Despite crashing in their first run, the Jamaican team crossed the finish line on foot to the applause of the crowd, proving that with passion and determination, any obstacle can be overcome.

These anecdotes serve as a reminder that the Olympic Games are more than just medals and records; they are a tapestry of human stories filled with moments of triumph, resilience, and unexpected twists and turns that make the Olympic spirit truly remarkable.

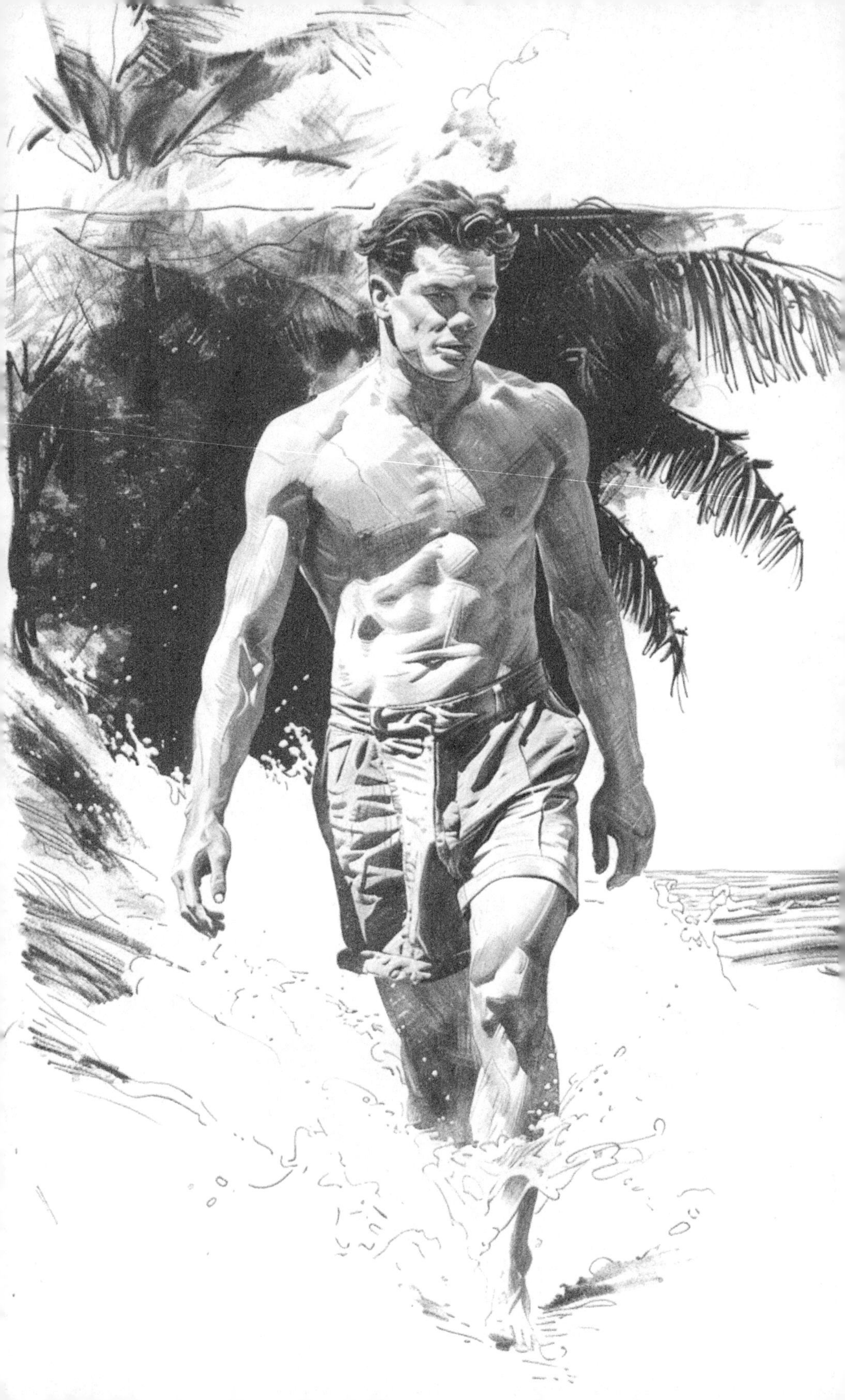

Olympic Athletes Who Became Movie Stars

Can you imagine your favorite Olympic stars also conquering the big screen? Well, it's not a dream! Throughout history, numerous athletes have shown that their talent and charisma are not limited to sports but can also shine in the world of cinema.

Esther Williams: The Hollywood Mermaid

In the pool: Won five gold medals at the Pan American Games and a bronze at the 1932 Los Angeles Olympics.

On the screen: She starred in over 30 films during the 1940s and 1950s, including "Bathing Beauty" (1948) and "Million Dollar Mermaid" (1952), becoming an icon of aquatic cinema.

Johnny Weissmuller: The King of the Jungle

In the pool: Won five gold medals at the

1924 and 1928 Olympic Games.

On the screen: He played Tarzan in 12 films between 1932 and 1948, becoming an icon of adventure cinema and the first talking Tarzan in film history.

Sonja Henie: The Ice Queen

On the ice: Won three gold medals at the 1928, 1932, and 1936 Olympic Games.

On the screen: A pioneer of ice skating in cinema, she starred in films such as "Iceland" (1942) and "Sun Valley Serenade" (1947), popularizing this sport.

Caitlyn Jenner: An Icon of Sports and the Transgender Community

On the track: Won the gold medal in decathlon at the 1976 Montreal Olympics.

On the screen and in life: She starred in the reality series "Keeping Up with the Kardashians" and became a visible figure in the transgender community, fighting for equality and acceptance.

Dara Torres: From the Waves to the Cameras

In the pool: Won four gold medals and four bronze medals in five Olympic Games between 1984 and 2000.

On the screen and in the pool: She has appeared in films such as "Baywatch" (1998) and "Blue Crush" (2002) as well as working as a commentator at sporting events.

Agyness Deyn: From the Snow to the Catwalk

On the snowboard: Competed in the 2002 Salt Lake City Winter Olympics.

On the catwalk and on the screen: After her sporting career, she became a successful model and has appeared in films such as "Clash of the Titans" (2010) and "Contagion" (2011).

Stephanie Rice: From the Pool to the Small Screen

In the pool: Won seven gold medals in three Olympic Games between 2004 and 2008.

On the screen and in the pool: She has appeared in television series such as "Home and Away" (2008) and works as an ambassador for various sports brands.

Allyson Felix: From the Track to the Big Screen

On the track: She has won 11 Olympic medals, six of them gold, between 2008 and 2020.

On the screen and on the track: She has appeared in films such as "Queen & Slim" (2019) and " Black-ish " (2021), as well as producing documentaries on social issues.

Thank You

Made in the USA
Middletown, DE
14 June 2024